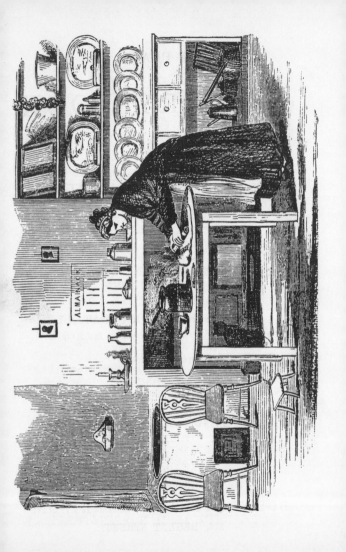

A PLAIN

COOKERY BOOK

FOR THE

WORKING CLASSES.

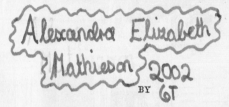

Alexandra Elizabeth Mathieson 2002

BY

6T

CHARLES ELMÉ FRANCATELLI,

LATE MAÎTRE D'HÔTEL AND CHIEF COOK TO HER MAJESTY THE
QUEEN. AUTHOR OF "THE MODERN COOK" AND
"THE COOK'S GUIDE."

Thursday 12th September 2002 While studing the Victorians.

LONDON:

BOSWORTH AND HARRISON,

215, REGENT STREET.

This copy of
A PLAIN COOKERY BOOK FOR THE WORKING CLASSES
is reproduced from an original copy of 1861 loaned
by Janet Clarke, antiquarian bookseller, specialist
in gastronomy, of Freshford, Bath

*Pryor Publications wish to thank
Peter Stockham for his advice and assistance
in the publication of this book.*

*Reprinted 1993 twice
Reprinted 1994
Reprinted 1995
Reprinted 1996
Reprinted 1997
Reprinted 1998
Reprinted 1999
Reprinted 2001
Reprinted 2002*

75 Dargate Road, Yorkletts, Whitstable
Kent CT5 3AE, England.
Tel & Fax: (01227) 274655

ISBN 0 946014 15 9

Printed by Thanet Press Limited, Margate, Kent

INTRODUCTION.

My object in writing this little book is to show you how you may prepare and cook your daily food, so as to obtain from it the greatest amount of nourishment at the least possible expense; and thus, by skill and economy, add, at the same time, to your comfort and to your comparatively slender means. The Recipes which it contains will afford sufficient variety, from the simple every-day fare to more tasty dishes for the birthday, Christmas-day, or other festive occasions.

In order to carry out my instructions properly, a few utensils will be necessary. Industry, good health, and constant employment, have, in many instances, I trust, enabled those whom I now address to lay by a little sum of money. A portion of this will be well spent in the purchase of the following articles:—A cooking-stove, with an oven at the side, or placed under the grate, which should be so planned as to admit of the fire being open or closed at will; by this contrivance much heat and fuel are economized; there should also be a boiler at the back of the grate. By this means you would have hot water always ready at hand, the advantage of which is considerable. Such poor men's cooking-stoves exist, on a large scale, in all modern-built lodging-houses. Also, a three-gallon iron pot with a lid to it, a one-gallon saucepan, a two-quart ditto, a frying-pan, a gridiron, and a strong tin baking-dish.

Here is a list of the cost prices at which the above-named articles, as well as a few others equally necessary, may be obtained of all ironmongers :—

	£	s.	d.
A cooking-stove, 2 ft. 6 in. wide, with oven only	1	10	0
Ditto, with oven and boiler . .	1	18	0
A three-gallon oval boiling pot . .	0	4	6
A one-gallon tin saucepan, and lid .	0	2	6
A two-quart ditto	0	1	6
A potato steamer	0	2	0
An oval frying-pan, from . . .	0	0	10
A gridiron, from	0	1	0
A copper for washing or brewing, twelve gallons	1	10	0
A mash-tub, from	0	10	0
Two cooling-tubs (or an old wine or beer cask cut in halves, would be cheaper, and answer the same purpose), each 6s. . . .	0	12	0
	£6	12	4

To those of my readers who, from sickness or

other hindrance, have not money in store, I would say, strive to lay by a little of your weekly wages to purchase these things, that your families may be well fed, and your homes made comfortable.

And now a few words on baking your own bread. I assure you if you would adopt this excellent practice, you would not only effect a great saving in your expenditure, but you would also insure a more substantial and wholesome kind of food; it would be free from potato, rice, bean or pea flour, and alum, all of which substances are objectionable in the composition of bread. The only utensil required for bread-baking would be a tub, or trough, capable of working a bushel or two of flour. This tub would be useful in brewing, for which you will find in this book plain and easy directions.

I have pointed out the necessity of procuring these articles for cooking purposes, and with the injunction to use great care in keeping them thoroughly clean, I will at once proceed to show you their value in a course of practical and economical cookery, the soundness and plainness of which I sincerely hope you will all be enabled to test in your own homes.

COOKERY BOOK.

No. 1. Boiled Beef. ✓

This is an economical dinner, especially where there are many mouths to feed; and consequently comes within the reach of your means. Buy a few pounds of either salt brisket, thick or thin flank, or buttock of beef; these pieces are always to be had at a low rate. Let us suppose you have bought a piece of salt beef for a Sunday's dinner, weighing about five pounds, at 6½d. per pound, that would come to 2s. 8½d.; two pounds of common flour, 4d., to be made into suet pudding or dumplings, and say 8½d. for cabbages, parsnips, and potatoes; altogether 3s. 9d. This would produce a substantial dinner for ten persons in family, and would, moreover, as children do not require much meat when they have pudding, admit of there being enough left to help out the next day's dinner, with potatoes.

No. 2. How to Boil Beef.

Put the beef into your three or four gallon pot, three parts filled with cold water, and set it on the fire to boil; remove all the scum that rises to the surface, and then let it boil gently on the hob; when the meat is about half done, which will take an hour, add the parsnips in a net, and at the end of another half hour put in the cabbages, also in a net. A piece of beef weighing five or six pounds will require about two hours' gentle boiling to cook it thoroughly. The dumplings may, of course, be boiled with the beef, etc. I may here observe that the dumplings and vegetables, with a small quantity of the meat, would be all-sufficient for the children's meal.

No. 3. Economical Pot Liquor Soup.

A thrifty housewife will not require that I should tell her to save the liquor in which the beef has been boiled; I will therefore take it for granted that the next day she carefully removes the grease, which will have become set firm on the top of the broth, into her fat pot, and keeps it to make a pie-crust, or to fry potatoes, or any remains of vegetables, onions, or fish. The liquor must be tasted, and if it is found to be too salt, some water must be added to lessen its saltness, and render it palatable. The pot containing the liquor must then be placed on the fire to boil, and when the scum rises to the surface it should be removed with a spoon. While the broth is boiling, put as many piled-up table-spoonfuls of oatmeal as you have pints of liquor into a basin; mix this with cold water into a smooth liquid batter, and then stir it into the boiling soup; season with some pepper and a good pinch of allspice, and continue stirring the soup with a stick or spoon on the fire for about twenty minutes; you will then be able to serve out a plentiful and nourishing meal to a large family at a cost of not more than the price of the oatmeal.

No. 4. Potato Soup for Six Persons.

Peel and chop four onions, and put them into a gallon saucepan, with two ounces of dripping fat, or butter, or a bit of fat bacon; add rather better than three quarts of water, and set the whole to boil on the fire for ten minutes; then throw in four pounds of peeled and sliced-up potatoes, pepper and salt, and with a wooden spoon stir the soup on the fire for about twenty-five minutes, by which time the potatoes will be done to a pulp, and the soup ready for dinner or breakfast.

No. 5. Pea Soup for Six Persons.

Cut up two and a-half pounds of pickled pork, or some pork cuttings, or else the same quantity of scrag end of neck of mutton, or leg of beef, and put any one of these kinds of meat into a pot with a gallon of water, three pints of split or dried peas, previously soaked in cold water over-night, two carrots, four onions, and a head of celery, all chopped small; season with pepper, but *no* salt, as the pork, if pork is used, will season the soup sufficiently; set the whole to boil very gently for at least three hours, taking care to skim it occasionally, and do not forget that the peas, etc., must be stirred from the bottom of the pot now and then; from three to four hours' gentle boiling will suffice to cook a good mess of this most excellent and satisfying soup. If fresh meat is used for this purpose, salt must be added to season it. Dried mint may be strewn over the soup when eaten.

No. 6. Onion Soup for Six Persons.

Chop fine six onions, and fry them in a gallon saucepan with two ounces of butter or dripping fat, stirring them continuously until they become of a very light colour; then add six ounces of flour or oatmeal, and moisten with three quarts of water; season with pepper and salt, and stir the soup while boiling for twenty minutes, and when done, pour it out into a pan or bowl containing slices of bread.

No. 7. Broth made from Bones for Soup.

Fresh bones are always to be purchased from butchers at about a farthing per pound; they must be broken up small, and put into a boiling-pot with a quart of water to every pound of bones; and being placed on the fire to boil, must be well skimmed, seasoned with pepper and salt, and a few carrots, onions, turnips, celery, and thyme, and boiled very gently for six hours; then to be strained off, and put back into the pot, with any bits of meat or gristle which may have fallen from the bones (the bones left are still worth a farthing per pound, and can be sold to the bone-dealers). Let this broth be thickened with peasemeal or oatmeal, in the proportion of a large table-spoonful to every pint of broth, and stirred over the fire while boiling for twenty-five minutes, by which time the soup will be done. It will be apparent to all good housewives that, with a little trouble and good management, a savoury and substantial meal may thus be prepared for a mere trifle.

No 8. Thick Milk for Breakfast.

Milk, buttermilk, or even skim-milk, will serve for this purpose. To every pint of milk, mix a piled-up table-spoonful of flour, and stir the mixture while boiling on the fire for ten minutes; season with a little salt, and eat it with bread or a boiled potato. This kind of food is well adapted for the breakfast of women and children, and is far preferable to a sloppy mess of tea, which comes to more money.

No. 9. Oatmeal Porridge for Six Persons.

To five pints of skim or buttermilk, add a couple of onions chopped fine, and set them to boil on the fire; meanwhile, mix six table-spoonfuls of oatmeal with a pint of milk or water very smoothly, pour it into the boiling milk and onions, and stir the porridge on the fire for ten minutes; season with salt to taste.

No. 10. Ox-cheek Soup.

An ox-cheek is always to be bought cheap; let it be thoroughly washed in several waters, place it whole in a three gallon boiling-pot filled up with water, and set it to boil on the fire; skim it well, season with carrots, turnips, onions, celery, allspice, pepper, and salt; and allow the whole to boil very gently by the side of the hob for about three hours and a-half, by which time the ox-cheek, etc., will be done quite tender; the cheek must then be taken out on to a dish, the meat removed from the bone, and after being cut up in pieces, put back into the soup again. Next mix smoothly twelve ounces of flour with a quart of cold water, pour this into the soup, and stir the whole on the fire, keeping it boiling for about twenty-five minutes longer; when it will be ready for dinner. One ox-cheek, properly managed, will, by attending to the foregoing instructions, furnish an ample quantity of substantial and nutritious food, equal to the wants of a large family, for three days' consumption.

No. 11. Sheep's-head Broth.

Get the butcher to split the sheep's head into halves, wash these clean, and put them into a boiling-pot with two gallons of water; set this on the fire to boil, skim it well, add carrots, turnips, onions, leeks, celery, thyme or winter savory, season with pepper and salt; add a pint of Patna rice, or Scotch barley; and allow the whole to keep gently boiling by the side of the fire for three hours, adding a little water to make up for the deficiency in quantity occasioned by boiling.

B

No. 12. Cow-heel Broth.

Put a couple of cow-heels into a boiling-pot, with a
pound of rice, a dozen leeks washed free from grit and
cut into pieces, and some coarsely chopped parsley;
fill up with six quarts of water, set the whole to boil
on the fire, skim it well, season with thyme, pepper,
and salt, and allow the whole to boil very gently on
the hob for about two hours. You will thus provide
a savoury meal at small cost.

No. 13. Bacon and Cabbage Soup.

When it happens that you have a dinner consisting of bacon and cabbages, you invariably throw away
the liquor in which they have been boiled, or, at the best,
give it to the pigs, if you possess any; this is wrong,
for it is easy to turn it to a better account for your
own use, by paying attention to the following instructions, viz.:—Put your piece of bacon on to boil in a
pot with two gallons (more or less, according to the
number you have to provide for) of water, and when
it has boiled up, and has been well skimmed, add the
cabbages, kale, greens, or sprouts, whichever may be
used, well washed and split down, and also some parsnips and carrots; season with pepper, but *no* salt, as
the bacon will season the soup sufficiently; and when
the whole has boiled together very gently for about
two hours, take up the bacon surrounded with the
cabbage, parsnips, and carrots, leaving a small portion
of the vegetables in the soup, and pour this into a
large bowl containing slices of bread; eat the soup
first, and make it a rule that those who eat most soup
are entitled to the largest share of bacon.

No. 14. Stewed Leg of Beef.

Four pounds of leg or shin of beef cost about one
shilling; cut this into pieces the size of an egg, and

fry them of a brown colour with a little dripping fat, in a good sized saucepan, then shake in a large handful of flour, add carrots and onions cut up in pieces the same as the meat, season with pepper and salt, moisten with water enough to cover in the whole, stir the stew on the fire till it boils, and then set it on the hob to continue boiling very gently for about an hour and a half, and you will then be able to enjoy an excellent dinner.

No. 15. Cocky Leeky.

I hope that at some odd times you may afford yourselves an old hen or cock; and when this occurs, this is the way in which I recommend that it be cooked, viz.:—First pluck, draw, singe off the hairs, and tie the fowl up in a plump shape; next, put it into a boiling-pot with a gallon of water, and a pound of Patna rice, a dozen leeks cut in pieces, some peppercorns and salt to season; boil the whole very gently for three hours, and divide the fowl to be eaten with the soup, which will prove not only nourishing but invigorating to the system.

No. 16. Roast Fowl and Gravy.

Let us hope that at Christmas, or some other festive season, you may have to dress a fowl or turkey for your dinner. On such occasions I would recommend the following method:—First, draw the fowl, reserving the gizzard and liver to be tucked under the wings; truss the fowl with skewers, and tie it to the end of a skein of worsted, which is to be fastened to a nail stuck in the chimney-piece, so that the fowl may dangle rather close to the fire, in order to roast it. Baste the fowl, while it is being roasted, with butter, or some kind of grease, and when nearly done, sprinkle it with a little flour and salt, and allow the fowl to attain a bright yellow-brown colour before you take it up. Then place it on its dish, and pour some brown gravy over it.

No. 17. This is the Brown Gravy for the Fowl.

Chop up an onion, and fry it with a sprig of thyme and a bit of butter, and when it is brown, add a good tea-spoonful of moist sugar and a drop of water, and boil all together on the fire until the water is reduced, and the sugar begins to bake of a dark brown colour. It must then be stirred on the fire for three minutes longer; after which moisten it with half-a-pint of water, add a little pepper and salt; boil all together for five minutes, and strain the gravy over the fowl, etc.

No. 18. Bread Sauce for a Roast Fowl.

Chop a small onion or shalot fine, and boil it in a pint of milk for five minutes; then add about ten ounces of crumb of bread, a bit of butter, pepper and salt to season; stir the whole on the fire for ten minutes, and eat this bread sauce with roast fowl or turkey.

No. 19. Egg Sauce for Roast Fowls, etc.

Boil two or three eggs for about eight minutes; remove the shells, cut up each egg into about ten pieces of equal size, and put them into some butter-sauce made as follows:—viz., Knead two ounces of flour with one ounce and-a-half of butter; add half-a-pint of water, pepper and salt to season, and stir the sauce on the fire until it begins to boil; then mix in the pieces of chopped hard-boiled eggs.

No. 20. Pork Chops, Grilled or Broiled.

Score the rind of each chop by cutting through the rind at distances of half-an-inch apart; season the chops with pepper and salt, and place them on a clean gridiron over a clear fire to broil; the chops must be turned over every two minutes until they are done; this will take about fifteen minutes. The chops are then to be eaten plain, or, if convenient, with brown gravy, made as shown in No. 17.

No. 21. SHARP SAUCE FOR BROILED MEATS.

Chop fine an onion and a pennyworth of mixed pickles; put these into a saucepan with half-a-gill of vinegar, a tea-spoonful of mustard, a small bit of butter, a large table-spoonful of bread-raspings, and pepper and salt to season; boil all together on the fire for at least six minutes; then add a gill of water, and allow the sauce to boil again for ten minutes longer. This sauce will give an appetizing fillip to the coarsest meats or fish when broiled or fried, and also when you are intending to make any cold meat into a hash or stew. In the latter case, the quantity of water and raspings must be doubled.

No. 22. ROAST VEAL, STUFFED.

A piece of the shoulder, breast, or chump-end of the loin of veal, is the cheapest part for you, and whichever of these pieces you may happen to buy, should be seasoned with the following stuffing:—To eight ounces of bruised crumb of bread add four ounces of chopped suet, shalot, thyme, marjoram, and winter savory, all chopped fine; two eggs, pepper and salt to season; mix all these ingredients into a firm compact kind of paste, and use this stuffing to fill a hole or pocket which you will have cut with a knife in some part of the piece of veal, taking care to fasten it in with a skewer. If you intend roasting the veal, and should not possess what is called a bottle-jack, nor even a Dutch oven, in that case the veal should be suspended by, and fastened to, the end of a twisted skein of worsted, made fast at the upper

end by tying it to a large nail driven into the centre
of the mantelpiece for that purpose. This contrivance will enable you to roast the veal by dangling
it before your fire; the exact time for cooking which,
must depend upon its weight. A piece of veal
weighing four pounds would require rather more
than an hour to cook it thoroughly before your
small fire.

No. 23. VEAL CUTLETS AND BACON.

You may sometimes have a chance to purchase a
few trimmings or cuttings of veal, or a small piece
from the chump end of the loin, which you can cut
up in thin slices, and after seasoning them with pepper
and salt, and rolling them in flour, they are to be fried
in the fat that remains from some slices of bacon which
you shall have previously fried; and, after placing the
fried veal and bacon in its dish, shake a table-spoonful
of flour in the frying-pan; add a few drops of ketchup
or vinegar and a gill of water; stir all together on the
fire to boil for five minutes, and pour this sauce over
the cutlets. A dish of cutlets of any kind of meat
may be prepared as above.

No. 24. A PUDDING MADE OF SMALL BIRDS.

Industrious and intelligent boys who live in the
country, are mostly well up in the cunning art of
catching small birds at odd times during the winter
months. So, my young friends, when you have been
so fortunate as to succeed in making a good catch of
a couple of dozen of birds, you must first pluck them
free from feathers, cut off their heads and claws, and
pick out their gizzards from their sides with the point
of a small knife, and then hand the birds over to your
mother, who, by following these instructions, will
prepare a famous pudding for your dinner or supper.
First, fry the birds whole with a little butter, shalot,

parsley, thyme, and winter savory, all chopped small, pepper and salt to season; and when the birds are half done, shake in a small handful of flour, add rather better than a gill of water, stir the whole on the fire while boiling for ten minutes, and when the stew of birds is nearly cold, pour it all into a good-sized pudding basin,.which has been ready-lined with either a suet and flour crust, or else a dripping-crust, cover the pudding in with a piece of the paste, and either bake or boil it for about an hour and-a-half.

No. 25. Baked Pig's Head.

Split the pig's head into halves, sprinkle them with pepper and salt, and lay them with the rind part uppermost upon a bed of sliced onions in a baking dish. Next bruise eight ounces of stale bread-crumb, and mix it with four ounces of chopped suet, twelve sage leaves chopped fine, pepper and salt to season, and sprinkle this seasoning all over the surface of the pig's head; add one ounce of butter and a gill of vinegar to the onions, and bake the whole for about an hour and-a-half, basting the pig's head occasionally with the liquor.

No. 26. Baked Goose.

Pluck and pick out all the stubble feathers thoroughly clean, draw the goose, cut off the head and neck, and also the feet and wings, which must be scalded to enable you to remove the pinion feathers from the wings and the rough skin from the feet; split and scrape the inside of the gizzard, and carefully cut out the gall from the liver. These giblets well stewed, as shown in No. 62, will serve to make a pie for another day's dinner. Next stuff the goose in manner following, viz.:—First put six potatoes to bake in t]:e oven, or even in a Dutch oven; and, while they are being baked, chop six onions with four apples and twelve sage leaves, and fry these in a saucepan with two ounces of butter, pepper and salt ; and, when the whole is slightly fried, mix it with the pulp from out of the inside of the six baked potatoes, and use this very nice stuffing to fill the inside of the goose. The goose being stuffed, place it upon an iron trivet in a baking dish containing peeled potatoes and a few apples ; add half-a-pint of water, pepper and salt, shake some flour over the goose, and bake it for about an hour and a-half.

No. 27. Baked Sucking Pigs.

Let the pig be stuffed in the same manner as directed for a goose, as shown in the preceding number ; score it all over crosswise, rub some grease or butter upon it, place it upon a trivet in a dish containing peeled potatoes and a few sliced onions, season with pepper and salt ; add half-a-pint of water, and bake the pig for about two hours, basting it frequently with its own dripping, or, a bit of butter tied up in a piece of muslin.

No. 28. Baked or Roast Ducks.

These are to be dressed in the same way as directed for dressing geese.

No. 29. How to make the most of a Pig, after it is killed.

Cottagers sometimes feed a pig for their own consumption, and therefore it is that, in the hope that many, if not all, of you may have it in your power to do so, I will give you proper instructions showing the best way to make the most of it. First, when the pig is killed, should the hair or bristles be wet, wipe them dry with a wisp of hay or straw, and having laid it on the ground upon a narrow bed of dry straw three inches in thickness, and laid some loose straw all over it, set fire to it, and as the upper straw burns out, lay on another covering of loose straw, and, by the time this has burnt out, all the hairs of the upper part of the pig will probably be singed off, if not, burn a little more straw upon the remaining parts; and, on turning the pig over, should it be found that any of the hairs yet remain, let them be singed off with a lighted wisp of straw. Throw a pail of water over the pig, and scrape it clean and dry with an old knife. The next thing to be done, is to insert a stout stick, pointed at the ends, into the hocks of the hind legs; fasten a strong cord to the stick, and hoist up the pig so as to enable you to stand up and finish your work with ease to yourself. With a sharp knife rip up the belly, and stretch out the flaps with two sticks to enable you to throw in some water to cleanse the pig's inside, having first removed the guts, etc.; hang up the pluck to cool, and also the chitterlings, and loose fat; and, after thoroughly wiping the pig, let it hang in the draught to become quite cold. You then split the pig in halves, commencing between the hind quarters; and, when this is done, first cut off the hocks, then the hams, and the head; next cleverly remove, slicing away, what is called the spare-rib—that is, the lean meat about the ribs—reaching up about four inches toward the breast part, and lay the spare-ribs aside to be sold or reserved for your own use. The head may be baked as shown in No. 25. The spare rib may be dressed as in No. 27.

No. 30. How to Cure Hams.

To six pounds of common salt, add four ounces of saltpetre, eight ounces of treacle, two ounces of salprunella, winter savory, bay-leaves, thyme, marjoram, and a good table-spoonful of allspice, bruise all these things well together, and thoroughly rub them over and into the hams, *with very clean hands*.

The rubbing-in must be repeated four or five successive mornings, and the hams must remain in this pickle for ten days longer.

No. 31. How to Smoke Hams.

When the hams have been well pickled, as shown in the preceding number, they must be pressed between boards with heavy stones to render them flat; the hams should remain in press for twenty-four hours; and, at the end of that time, must be well rubbed all over with peasemeal mixed with a little salt; and are then to be smoked in a close shed or in the chimney, burning for that purpose some branches of juniper or any other wood, and some sawdust. The smoking must last five days. The hams, when sufficiently smoked, must be kept in a cool place. They will not be ripe for cooking before six months after their curing. Remember that a couple of well-cured hams, kept in reserve for a case of need, will always prove a ready means to realize some twenty-five shillings towards paying the rent, etc.

No. 32. How to Cure Bacon.

Mind that your pickling-trough is well scalded out before using it for pickling the bacon. Allow at the rate of four ounces of salt to every pound of meat, and to every ten pounds of salt six ounces of saltpetre, two ounces of salprunella, and eight ounces of sugar; rub the salt, etc., well into the bacon every morning for twelve successive days; and at the end of that time, let the sides of bacon be pressed between boards with heavy stones placed upon them to keep them flat; and at the end of twenty-four hours, rub them over with peasemeal in which there has been mixed a little salt, and smoke the bacon in the same manner as the hams; and thus, by timely thriftiness, you will be provided with a meat dinner for a long while.

No. 33. How to dispose of the Pig's Pluck.

See Nos. 72 and 73.

No. 34. How to make Pork Sausages.

Take equal parts of fat and lean meat, such as, for instance, the inferior end of the spare-ribs and some of the loose fat; chop these well together, adding a few sage leaves and a little thyme, pepper and salt, and one or two eggs; and, when the whole is thoroughly mixed and chopped fine, then use a sprinkle of flour on a table or dresser, for the purpose of rolling the sausages into shape of the size and form of a man's thumb. These sausages may be fried in the ordinary way.

No. 35. Black Puddings.

When a pig is killed, the blood should be caught in a pan, and a little salt must be stirred in with it while yet warm, to prevent its coagulation or thickening. This will serve to make you some hog's puddings, an excellent thing in its way, and for the preparation of which you must attend to the following instructions, viz.:—To every pound of blood, add eight ounces of fat cut up in small squares, two ounces of rice or grits, boiled quite soft in milk; season with pepper and salt, chopped sage, thyme, and winter savory, and some chopped onions boiled soft in a little milk or water; mix all these things well together, and use a tin funnel for filling in the cleansed guts with the preparation, taking care to tie the one end of each piece of gut with string, to prevent waste. The puddings being filled in with the preparation, tie them in links, each pudding measuring about six inches in length, and when all are tied, let them be dropped into a pot containing boiling-water, just taken off the fire, and allow them to remain in this until they become set, or slightly firm; the puddings must then be carefully lifted out, and hung to a nail driven into the wall, to drain free from all excess of moisture; and before they are fried or broiled, they must be slightly scored with a sharp knife, to prevent them from bursting while they are being cooked.

No. 36. How to Melt down the Seam, or Loose Fat.

Cut up the seam in small pieces, put it in a pot with about a gill of water, and set it over a slow fire to melt down, stirring it frequently with a spoon to prevent it from burning; and as soon as all is melted, let it be strained off into a jar for use. This will produce what is called lard, and will serve for making lard cakes, pie or pudding crusts, and also for general cooking purposes, instead of butter, etc.

No. 37. Italian Cheese.

This is prepared by chopping up the whole of the pig's pluck, the chitterlings, and a couple of pounds of the fat; mix this in a pan with seasoning composed of chopped sage, thyme, winter savory, allspice, pepper, and salt, and with it fill earthen pots or jars having lids to them; bake the contents in moderate heat; or if you have no oven of your own, send them to the baker's. A jar containing two pounds would require about an hour and three-quarters' baking. Italian cheese is to be eaten cold, spread upon bread.

No. 38. Pig's Feet.

These are to be well salted for about four days, and then boiled in plenty of water for about three hours, and may be eaten either hot or cold.

No. 39. Curried Rice.

Boil one or more pounds of rice, as directed in No.

92, and drain all the water from it ; slice some onions very thin, and fry them brown with a little butter ; then add the boiled rice, a spoonful of curry-powder, and a little salt to season ; mix all together. This is excellent with boiled or fried fish.

No. 40. A Plain Rice Pudding.

To every quart of milk add six ounces of rice, one ounce of brown sugar, a pinch of allspice, and ditto of salt ; put all these in a proper sized pie-dish, with one ounce of butter, and set the pudding to bake for one hour and-a-half. When the pudding has been in the oven half an hour, stir it round with a fork.

No. 41. A Ground Rice Pudding.

Ingredients, eight ounces of ground rice, three pints of skim milk, one ounce of butter, four ounces of sugar, a pinch of allspice or bit of lemon-peel, a pinch of salt, and two or three eggs ; mix all the above ingredients (except the eggs) in a saucepan, and stir them on the fire till the batter boils ; then beat up the eggs with a fork in a basin, and mix them well into the rice batter, and pour the whole into a well-greased pie-dish, and bake the pudding for an hour.

No. 42. A Bread Pudding for a Family.

Ingredients, a two-pound loaf, two quarts of milk, two ounces of butter, four ounces of sugar, four ounces of plums or currants, three eggs, a piece of lemon-peel chopped, and a spoonful of salt. Divide the loaf into four equal-sized pieces, and soak them in boiling-water for twenty minutes, then squeeze out the water, and put the bread into a saucepan with the milk, butter, sugar, lemon-peel, and salt, and stir all together on the fire till it boils ; next add the beaten eggs and the currants ; pour the pudding into a proper sized greased baking-dish, and bake it for an hour and a-quarter.

No. 43. A Batter and Fruit Pudding.

Ingredients, two quarts of milk, one pound of flour, four eggs, eight ounces of sugar, one quart of fruit (either plums, gooseberries, currants, &c.), one ounce of butter, a good pinch of salt. First, mix the flour, eggs, sugar, salt, and a pint of the milk, by working all together in a basin or pan, with a spoon, and when quite smooth, add the remainder of the milk ; work the batter thoroughly, and pour it into a large pie-dish, greased with the butter ; add the fruit, and bake the pudding for an hour and a-quarter.

No. 44. A Treacle Pudding.

Ingredients, two pounds of flour, twelve ounces of treacle, six ounces of suet or dripping fat, a quarter of an ounce of baking-powder. a pinch of allspice, a little salt, one pint of milk, or water. Mix the whole of the above-named ingredients in a pan, into a firm compact paste ; tie it up in a well-greased and floured pudding-cloth ; boil the pudding for at least two hours and a-half, and when done, cut it in slices, and pour a little sweetened melted butter over it.

No. 45. Apple Pudding.

Ingredients, one pound and a-half of flour, six ounces of suet chopped fine, two pounds of peeled apples, four ounces of sugar, a little salt, and three gills of water. Mix the flour, suet, and salt with three quarters of a pint of water into a firm paste ; roll this out with flour shaken over the table, using a rolling-pin to roll it out ; and line a greased cloth, which you have spread in a hollow form within a large basin, with the rolled-out paste ; fill up the hollow part of the paste with the peeled apples, gather up the sides of the paste in a purse-like form, and twist them firmly together; tie up the pudding in the cloth, boil it in plenty of boiling water for two hours, and when it is turned out of the cloth on to its dish, cut out a round piece from the top, and stir in the sugar.

No. 46. RICE AND APPLES.

Ingredients, one pound of rice, twelve apples, two ounces of sugar. Tie up the rice very loose in a pudding-cloth, so as to admit that while boiling it may have sufficient room to swell out to five times its original quantity. While the rice is boiling, which will take about one hour, peel the apples, and put them in a saucepan with nearly half-a-pint of water, a bit of butter, lemon-peel, and the sugar, and stew them on the fire till dissolved, stirring them while boiling for a few minutes. When your rice pudding is done and turned out on its dish, pour the apple-sauce over it. This cheap kind of rice pudding may also be eaten with all kinds of fruits, prepared in the same manner as herein directed for apples.

No. 47. BROWN AND POLSON PUDDING.

Ingredients, six ounces of Brown and Polson's prepared Indian corn, two quarts of milk, two ounces of sugar, a bit of cinnamon or lemon-peel, a pinch of salt, three eggs. Mix all the above ingredients (except the eggs) in a saucepan, and stir them on the fire till they come to a boil; then add the eggs beat up; mix thoroughly, pour the batter into a pie-dish greased with butter, and bake the pudding for one hour. Brown and Polson's prepared Indian corn is a most excellent and economical article of food, equal to arrow-root, and will prove, on trial, to be both substantial and nutritive, and also easy of digestion to the most delicate stomachs.

No. 48. Brown and Polson Fruit Pudding.

Prepare the pudding batter as indicated in the foregoing number, and when you have poured one-half of it into the greased pie-dish, strew about two pounds of any kind of fruit upon this, such as goose-berries, currants, plums, cherries, etc., and then pour the remainder of the batter all over the fruit. Bake the pudding an hour and a quarter. Peeled apples or pears may be used for the same purpose.

No. 49. Brown and Polson Thick Milk.

Ingredients, three ounces of Brown and Polson's prepared Indian corn, one quart of milk, one ounce of sugar, a bit of cinnamon, a pinch of salt. Mix all the above-named ingredients together in a saucepan, and stir them constantly while boiling on the fire for ten minutes. This thick milk is most excellent for children's breakfast or supper, and would be found both cheaper and better for their health than a sloppy mess of tea.

No. 50. Potato Pudding.

Ingredients, three pounds of potatoes, two quarts of milk, two ounces of butter, two ounces of sugar, a bit of lemon-peel, a good pinch of salt, and three eggs. First, bake the potatoes, and if you have no means of baking them, let them be either steamed or boiled, and when done, scoop out all their floury pulp without waste into a large saucepan, and immediately beat it up vigorously with a large fork or a spoon; then add all the remainder of the above-named ingredients (excepting the eggs), stir the potato batter carefully on the fire till it comes to a boil, then add the beaten eggs; pour the batter into a greased pie-dish, and bake the pudding for an hour in your oven, if you have one; if not, send it to the baker's.

No. 51. YEAST DUMPLINGS.

Ingredients, two pounds of flour, a halfpenny worth of yeast, a pinch of salt, one pint of milk or water. Put the flour in a pan, with your fist hollow out a hole in the centre of the flour, place the yeast and salt at the bottom, then add the milk (which should be lukewarm), and with your clean hand gradually mix the whole well together, and work the dough perfectly smooth and elastic. The pan containing the dough must then be covered over with a cloth, and in the winter must be placed on a stool in a corner near the fire, that it may rise, or increase in size to nearly double its original quantity. When the dough has risen in a satisfactory manner, which will take about an hour, dip your hand in some flour and work it, or rather knead it together, without allowing it to stick to your hands ; divide it into about twelve equal parts ; roll these with flour into balls, and as you turn them out of hand, drop them gently into a pot on the fire, half full of *boiling* water ; allow the water to boil up once as you drop each dumpling in separately, before you attempt to put in another, in order to prevent the dumplings from sticking together, as this accident would produce a very unsatisfactory result, and spoil your dinner. Yeast dumplings must not boil too fast, as then they might boil out of the pot. They will require about half-an-hour's boiling to cook them ; they must be eaten immediately, with a little butter or dripping, and salt or sugar.

No. 52. NORFOLK DUMPLINGS.

Ingredients, two pounds of flour, a pint of milk, a good pinch of salt. Let all these ingredients be well mixed in a pan, and after dividing the paste into twelve equal parts, roll these into balls, drop each of

c

them into a pot half full of *boiling* water on the fire,
and allow the dumplings to continue boiling rather
fast for half-an-hour, at the end of which time they
will be done. They should then be eaten while hot,
with a little butter or dripping, and either sugar,
treacle, or salt. Norfolk dumplings are also most
excellent things to eke out an insufficient supply of
baked meat for the dinner of a large family of children.

No. 53. STEWED EELS.

First skin, gut, and trim away the fins from the
eels, and then cut them into pieces three inches long;
put these into a saucepan, add a bit of butter, a
spoonful of flour, some chopped parsley, pepper and
salt, a little mushroom ketchup, and enough water to
cover the pieces of eel; put them on the fire to boil
gently for about ten minutes, shaking them round in
the saucepan occasionally until they are done.

No. 54. STEWED OYSTERS.

Put the oysters, with their liquor and a little water
or milk, into a saucepan; add a bit of butter kneaded,
that is, well mixed with a table-spoonful of flour;
pepper, and a little salt; stir the oysters over the
fire until they have gently boiled for about five minutes,
and then pour them into a dish containing some slices
of toasted bread.

No. 55. STEWED MUSCLES, OR MUSSELS.

Thoroughly wash the muscles, and pull off any
weeds there may be hanging to them; next put them in
a clean saucepan with a little water, and salt enough to
season, and set them on the fire to boil, tossing them
occasionally, until you find that their shells begin to
open; they must then be taken off the fire, and their
liquor poured off into a basin. Next, after removing
one of the shells from each muscle, put them back into

the saucepan; add the liquor, a bit of butter, a spoonful of flour, some pepper, chopped parsley, and a little drop of vinegar, toss the whole over the fire until the muscles have boiled five minutes, and then you will enjoy a treat for supper. Cockles and whelks are cooked in the same way.

No. 56. Baked Beef and Potatoes.

The cheapest pieces of beef, suitable for baking or roasting, consist of the thick part of the ribs, cut from towards the shoulder, the mouse buttock and gravy pieces, and also what is commonly called the chuck of beef, which consists of the throat boned and tied up with string in the form of a small round. Whichever piece of beef you may happen to buy should be well sprinkled over with pepper and salt and flour, and placed upon a small iron trivet in a baking dish containing peeled potatoes and about half-a-pint of water, and either baked in your own oven or else sent to the baker's. If you bake your meat in your own oven, remember that it must be turned over on the trivet every twenty minutes, and that you must be careful to baste it all over now and then with the fat which runs from it into the dish, using a spoon for that purpose. It would be very economical if, when you have baked meat for dinner, you were always to make a Yorkshire pudding to be baked under it. There are baking dishes made with a parting down the middle which just suit this purpose. In this case the potatoes are put in one part and the pudding in the other part.

No. 57. Yorkshire Pudding.

To one pound of flour add three pints of skim milk, two eggs, nutmeg and salt; mix smoothly, and pour the pudding into the greased dish, and bake it under the meat, as recommended above.

No. 58. Baked Suet Pudding.

To one pound of flour add six ounces of chopped suet, three pints of skim milk, nutmeg and salt; mix thoroughly and smoothly, and bake the pudding in the dish under the meat.

No. 59. Toad in the Hole.

To make this a cheap dinner, you should buy 6d. or 1s. worth of bits or pieces of any kind of meat, which are to be had cheapest at night when the day's sale is over. The pieces of meat should be first carefully overlooked, to ascertain if there be any necessity to pare away some tainted part, or perhaps a fly-blow, as this, if left on any one piece of meat, would tend to impart a bad taste to the whole, and spoil the dish. You then rub a little flour, pepper, and salt all over the meat, and fry it brown with a little butter or fat in the frying-pan, and when done, put it with the fat it has been fried in into a baking-dish containing some Yorkshire or suet pudding batter, made as directed at Nos. 57 and 58, and bake the toad-in-the-hole for about an hour and a half, or else send it to the baker's.

No. 60. Boiled Shoulder of Mutton with Onions.

Put the shoulder of mutton to boil in your two-gallon pot, with a handful of salt and plenty of water, allow it to boil gently for about two hours, and when done, and placed on its dish, smother it over with the following sauce:—Chop six or eight large onions, and boil them with a pint of water for twenty minutes, by which time the water must be reduced to half a pint; then add two ounces of butter, a pint of milk, four ounces of flour, pepper, and salt, and stir the sauce whilst boiling for ten minutes. A shoulder of mutton for boiling is all the better for its being salted for two or three days previous to its being cooked.

No. 61. Meat Pie.

Of whatever kind, let the pieces of meat be first fried brown over a quick fire, in a little fat or butter, and seasoned with pepper and salt; put these into a pie-dish with chopped onions, a few slices of half-cooked potatoes, and enough water just to cover the meat. Cover the dish with a crust, made with two pounds of flour and six ounces of butter, or lard, or fat dripping, and just enough water to knead it into a stiff kind of dough or paste, and then bake it for about an hour and a-half.

No. 62. Giblet Pie.

Giblets of fowls are always to be bought at a low price at most poulterers'; when you have a mind to lay out 6d. or 1s. in this way, first scald the necks and feet, to remove the feathers from the head and the rough skin from the feet; split the gizzard and scrape out the stones, etc., and the yellow skin therefrom, and when the giblets are thoroughly cleaned, put them into a saucepan with some thyme, winter savory, chopped onions, pepper and salt, and about a quart of water, and set them on the fire to stew very gently for an hour, by which time the liquor should be boiled down to half that quantity; then add two ounces of flour and a little mushroom ketchup; stir all together, and put the giblets into a pie-dish; cover this over with a dripping crust, and bake it for about an hour and a quarter.

No. 63. A Fish Pie.

Cut up any kind of fish into pieces the size of an egg; season these with chopped parsley, thyme, a little onion, pepper and salt, and put them into

a pie-dish, with a pint of water, well mixed with three
ounces of flour and a little mushroom ketchup; cover
the pie with a flour crust, or else with stiff mashed
potatoes, and bake it for an hour and a quarter.

No. 64. POTATO PIE.

Slice up four onions and boil them in a saucepan
with two ounces of butter, a quart of water, and pepper
and salt, for five minutes; then add four pounds of
potatoes, peeled and cut in slices; stew the whole
until the potatoes are done, and pour them into a pie-
dish; cover this with stiff mashed potatoes, and bake
the pie of a light brown colour.

No. 65. BACON ROLL-PUDDING.

Boil a pound of fat bacon for half an hour, and
then cut it up into thin slices. Peel six apples and
one onion, and cut them in slices. Make two pounds
of flour into a stiff dough, roll it out thin; first
lay the slices of bacon out all over this, and then upon
the slices of bacon spread out the slices of apples and
the slices of onion; roll up the paste so as to secure
the bacon, etc., in it, and place the bolster pudding
in a cloth, to be rolled up in it, tied at each end, and
boiled for two hours in a two-gallon pot, with plenty
of water.

No. 66. RABBIT PUDDING.

Skin and wash the rabbit, and cut it up in pieces;
fry these brown with a bit of butter, season with
chopped onions, parsley, and winter savory, pepper and
salt, shake in a good spoonful of flour, moisten with a
little ketchup and a gill of water; toss the saucepan about on the fire while the pieces of rabbit boil
for about ten minutes, and then pour the whole into
a proper sized basin lined with a suet or dripping
crust; let the pudding be covered in with some of the

paste, put into a baking-dish half full of hot water, and placed in the oven, to bake for an hour and a-half.

No. 67. STEWED OX KIDNEY.

Cut up the kidney in thin slices, fry them brown with a bit of butter or fat in a frying-pan, over a brisk fire, season with chopped parsley, shalot, pepper and salt, shake in a good table-spoonful of flour, add a few drops of vinegar, and nearly half a pint of water, and stir the whole on the fire, while it boils, very gently, for a quarter of an hour; and this, with a dish of well-boiled or baked potatoes, will produce a cheap and excellent dinner sufficient for six persons.

No. 68. BAKED BULLOCK'S HEART.

Wash and wipe the heart, cut it into four pieces, season these with pepper and salt, chopped thyme, and bay-leaves, add about two ounces of dripping, eight onions cut in slices, and four parsnips cut also in slices; let all this be placed in an earthen pot, with a pint of water, and the lid being put on, set the stew in the oven to bake for two hours.

No. 69. BULLOCK'S HEART STUFFED.

Chop fine four onions and twelve sage-leaves, and put these in a saucepan with a bit of fat or butter, and fry them for a few minutes on the fire; then add eight ounces of crumb of bread, soaked in milk or water, pepper and salt; stir this stuffing on the fire for a few minutes, add one egg, put the stuffing inside the bullock's heart, place a round of greased paper on the stuffing, and fasten it on with four wooden twigs. Next, put the stuffed heart upon an iron trivet in a baking dish, containing peeled potatoes, two ounces of dripping or butter, and half a pint of water; season well with pepper and salt, and while baking let the heart be frequently basted with the fat from the dish. In case you have no oven, send it to the baker's.

No. 70. STEWED SHEEP'S TROTTERS.

Sheep's trotters are sold ready cleaned and very cheap at all tripe shops. When about to cook them, by way of a treat, for supper, or otherwise, let them be put on in two quarts of water and milk, seasoned with peppercorns, salt, a good sprig of thyme, and a wine-glassful of vinegar, and set them to boil very gently on the fire for three hours, at least. When the trotters are done quite tender, skim off all the grease, and boil down the liquor to a pint; then add two ounces of flour, mixed with a gill of milk, some chopped parsley, and one ounce of butter; stir all together while boiling on the fire for ten minutes, and pour out into the dish.

No. 71. BAKED SHEEP'S HEADS.

Buy a couple of sheep's heads, get the butcher to split them for you, place them in an earthen baking-dish, with two ounces of dripping, some chopped shalots, thyme, bay-leaf, winter savory, pepper and salt, and a good pinch of allspice; moisten with a quart of cider, or water, strew a coating of bread-raspings all over the surface of the heads, and bake them for two hours.

No. 72. SHEEP'S PLUCK.

A sheep's pluck, properly cooked, will furnish a meat dinner enough for twelve persons, at a very moderate cost. Cut the whole of the pluck, consisting of the heart, liver, lights, etc., into rather thick slices, and season them well with pepper, salt, allspice, thyme, and winter savory; grease the bottom of a baking-dish with two ounces of dripping, lay a bed of slices of onions upon this, and then place the slices of pluck, already seasoned, upon the onions; moisten with water enough to reach half-way up the meat, strew a thick coating of bread-raspings all over the top, and bake the savoury mess for an hour and a-half.

No. 73. BELGIAN FAGGOTS.

These may be prepared with sheep's pluck, or even with bullock's liver, and other similar parts of meat; but a pig's pluck is preferable for the purpose. Chop up the heart, liver, lights, and the fat crow; season well with pepper, salt, allspice, thyme, sage, and shalots, and divide this sausage-meat into balls the size of an apple, which must be each secured in shape with a piece of pig's caul fastened with a wooden twig, or skewer, and placed in rows in a tin baking-dish, to be baked for about half an hour in a brisk oven. When the faggots are done, place them on some well-boiled cabbages, chopped up, in an earthen dish, and having poured the grease from the faggots over all, set them in the oven to stew gently for half an hour.

No. 74. FRIED STEAKS AND ONIONS.

Season the steaks with pepper and salt, and when done brown on both sides, without being overdone, place them in a dish before the fire while you fry some sliced onions in the fat which remains in the pan; and as soon as the onions are done, and added to the steaks, shake a spoonful of flour in the pan, add a gill of water and a few drops of vinegar; give this gravy a boil up on the fire, and pour it over the steaks, etc.

No. 75. STEWED STEAKS.

Fry the steaks brown over a very brisk fire, without allowing them to be hardly half done, and place them in a saucepan with onions, carrots, turnips, and celery, all cut in pieces about the size of a pigeon's egg; season with thyme, pepper, and salt, and two ounces of flour; moisten with a quart of water, and stir the stew on the fire till it boils, and then set it by the side of the fire on the hob, to simmer very gently for an hour and a-half. It will then be ready for dinner.

No. 76. STEWED SAUSAGES.

First, prick your sausages well all over with a fork, and soak them in very hot water, for two or three minutes, to swell them out; next, roll them in flour, and fry them brown without overdoing them, as that renders them dry, and spoils them. When the sausages are done and put on a plate, fry some slices of bread, and put these on a dish; then put the sausages on the fried bread, and shake a spoonful of flour in the pan; add a pennyworth of chopped mixed pickles, a gill of water, and a little pepper and salt; give this gravy a boil up, and pour it over the sausages.

No. 77. PIG'S FRY.

A pig's fry consists of the heart, liver, lights, and some of the chitterlings; these are to be first cut up in slices, then seasoned with pepper and salt, rolled in a little flour, and fried with some kind of grease in the frying-pan. As the pieces are fried, place them on their dish to keep hot before the fire, and when all is done, throw some chopped onions and sage leaves into the pan, to be fried of a light colour; add a very little flour, pepper, and salt, a gill of water, and a few drops of vinegar; boil up this gravy, and pour it over the pig's fry.

No. 78. BEEFSTEAKS, PLAIN.

When you happen to have a clear fire, the steaks may be cooked on a gridiron over the fire; the steaks must be turned on the gridiron every two or three minutes. This precaution assists very much in rendering the meat more palatable and tender, as it is by this frequent turning over of the meat while broiling, that the juices are not allowed to run off in waste, but are re-absorbed by the meat. When the steaks are cooked, rub them over with a small bit of butter, season with pepper and salt. A little chopped shalot sprinkled over steaks, imparts an extra relish.

No. 79. Mutton Chops, or Steaks.

Mutton chops, properly speaking, are an expensive affair; but what I recommend you to buy is, the chump end of the loin of mutton, which is always to be had much cheaper. This weighs about one pound, at 6*d.*, and would cut into about three, or perhaps four steaks or chops; let these be broiled in the same manner as recommended for beefsteaks.

No. 80. Kidney Pudding.

Prepare an ox kidney as shown in No. 67, and use this to fill a good sized pudding basin, which you shall have previously lined with a dripping or suet crust; cover the meat in by placing a rolled-out piece of the paste on the top, fasten it by pressing the two edges of the paste together, tie the pudding up in a cloth, and take care to place the bottom of the pudding-basin downward in the pot in which it is to be boiled. It will take about two hours to boil a good sized pudding of this kind; and when you take it up out of the pot, be very careful not to run the fork through the crust, and pay great attention how you handle the pudding while removing the cloth, so as not to spill or waste the gravy it contains, as that would go very far towards spoiling the pudding you have had all the trouble to prepare.

No. 81. Hashed Meats.

I strongly recommend that you never allow your

selves to be persuaded that cold meat dinners are cheap dinners; just the reverse of this assumption is the fact. And, let me tell you, that those who make the former assertion, do so only because they know no better, and as an excuse for their idleness. I am well aware that in your homes it is not a common every-day occurrence for you to dress a large joint of meat, from which enough would be left for one or more days' dinner; but still it may, and does sometimes occur, that you have cold meat at your disposal, upon which you may exercise your knowledge in domestic economy. Besides, some of you who are living close to noblemen and gentlemen's mansions in the country, or otherwise, may perhaps stand a chance of now and then receiving a donation of this kind. And whenever you have any cold meat, I advise you to cook it up into stews of the various kinds described in this work, or else make it into a hash as follows: First, chop two onions fine, and put them to boil with pepper and salt and a pint of water, in a saucepan for ten minutes, then throw in the meat cut in thin slices, mixed with a little flour; boil all together gently for ten minutes longer, and pour the hash into a dish containing either some ready boiled potatoes, or else some slices of toasted bread.

No. 82. Boiled Tripe.

Tripe is not exactly a cheap commodity for food; yet. as you may feel occasionally inclined to indulge in a treat of this kind, I will give you instructions to cook it in the most economical manner. When you have procured any given quantity of tripe, cut it up in pieces the size of two inches square, put these into a saucepan containing skim milk, or milk and water, enough to swim the tripe; add some peeled onions, pepper, and salt, and a sprig of thyme, and boil gently for at least an hour; and when the tripe is done, eat it with mustard and some well boiled potatoes.

No. 83. BAKED TRIPE.

Cut the tripe up in pieces, and put it into an earthen pot, with some ale. cider, or water, enough to cover it in; add sliced onions. pepper, and salt, and a good pinch of allspice; put the lid on the pot, and set the tripe in the oven to bake for two hours.

No. 84. SAUSAGE DUMPLINGS.

Make one pound of flour and two ounces of dripping, or chopped suet, into a firm paste, by adding just enough water to enable you to knead the whole together. Divide this paste into twelve equal parts, roll each of these out sufficiently large to be able to fold up one of the beef sausages in it, wet the edge of the paste to fasten the sausage securely in it, and, as you finish off each sausage dumpling, drop it gently into a large enough saucepan, containing plenty of *boiling* water, and when the whole are finished, allow them to boil gently by the side of the fire for one hour, and then take up the dumplings with a spoon free from water, on to a dish, and eat them while they are hot.

No. 85. SAUSAGE ROLLS.

Procure a quartern of dough from the baker's, knead this with four ounces of butter, dripping, or chopped suet; divide it into twelve equal parts, and use each piece of paste to enfold a beef sausage in it; place these rolls on a baking-tin, and bake them in the oven for about twenty minutes to half an hour.

No. 86. ROAST PORK.

Let us suppose, or rather hope, that you may

sometimes have a leg of pork to cook for your dinner; it will eat all the better if it is scored all over by cutting the rind. or rather slitting it crosswise, at short distances, with the point of a sharp knife; it is to be well sprinkled all over with salt, and allowed to absorb the seasoning during some hours previously to its being cooked. Prepare some stuffing as follows:—Chop six onions and twelve sage leaves fine, fry these with a bit of butter, pepper, and salt, for five minutes; then add six ounces of bread soaked in water; stir all together on the fire for five minutes, and use this stuffing to fill up a hole or pocket, which you will make by running the point of a knife down between the rind and the flesh of the joint of pork; secure this by sewing it up, or else fasten it securely in with a small wooden skewer or twig. The joint of pork, so far prepared, must then be placed upon a trivet in a baking-dish containing plenty of peeled potatoes, and, if possible, a few apples for the children; add half a pint of water, pepper and salt, and if the joint happens to be a leg, it will require about two hours to bake it.

No. 87. Bubble and Squeak.

When you happen to have some cold boiled salt beef, cut this up in slices, and fry it on both sides, and dish it up round some cabbages and any dressed vegetables ready to hand, which must be chopped up, seasoned with pepper and salt, and fried.

No. 88. Jugged Hare.

It does sometimes happen that when you are living in the country, in the neighbourhood of considerate gentlefolks who possess game preserves. that they now and then make presents of a hare and a few rabbits to the poor cottagers in their vicinity. And when you are so fortunate as to have a hare given to you, this is the way to cook it:—First, cut the hare up into pieces of equal size, then cut up a pound of bacon into small squares, and fry these in a saucepan for five minutes; next, add the pieces of hare, and, stirring them round in the pot with a spoon, fry them brown; add a good handful of flour, some pepper and allspice, carrots and onions, and a sprig of winter savory; moisten the stew with nearly three pints of water, and stir it all together on the fire till it boils, and then set it on the hob to continue gently simmering for about an hour and a-half or two hours; the jugged hare will then be ready for dinner.

No. 89. Boiled Bacon and Cabbages.

Put a piece of bacon in a pot capable of containing two gallons; let it boil up, and skim it well; then put in some well-washed split cabbages, a few carrots and parsnips also split, and a few peppercorns, and when the whole has boiled gently for about an hour and a-half, throw in a dozen peeled potatoes, and by the time that these are done, the dinner will be ready. And this is the way in which to make the most of this excellent and economical dinner. First, take up the bacon, and having placed it on its dish, garnish it round with the cabbages, carrots, parsnips, and potatoes, and then add some pieces of crust, or thin slices of bread, to the liquor in which the bacon-dinner has been cooked, and this will furnish you with a good wholesome soup with which to satisfy the first peremptory call of your healthy appetites.

No. 90. Economical Vegetable Pottage.

In France, and also in many parts of Europe, the poorer classes but very seldom taste meat in any form; the chief part of their scanty food consists of bread, vegetables, and more especially of their soup, which is mostly, if not entirely, made of vegetables, or, as is customary on the southern coasts of France, Italy, and Spain, more generally of fish, for making which kinds of soup see Nos. 4, 6, 118, etc.

The most common as well as the easiest method for making a good mess of cheap and nutritious soup is the following:—If you are five or six in family, put a three-gallon pot on the fire rather more than half full of water, add four ounces of butter, pepper and salt, and small sprigs of winter savory, thyme, and parsley; and when this has boiled, throw in any portion or quantity. as may best suit your convenience, of such of the following vegetables as your garden can afford:—Any kind of cabbages cleaned and split, carrots, turnips, parsnips, broad beans, French beans, peas, broccoli, red cabbages, vegetable marrow, young potatoes, a few lettuce, some chervil, and a few sprigs of mint. Allow all this to simmer by the side of the hob for about two hours, and then, after taking up the more considerable portion of the whole vegetables on to a dish, eat one half, or as much as you may require, of the soup with bread in it, and make up your dinner with the whole vegetables and more bread. The remainder will serve for the next day. Let me persuade you, my friends, to try and persevere in adopting this very desirable kind of food, when in your power, for your ordinary fare. I, of course, intend this remark more particularly for the consideration of such of my readers as are or may be located in the country, and who may have a little garden of their own.

No. 91. How to make a Fish Curry.

Slice up six onions fine, and fry them with a little butter or grease over a slow fire until they become very lightly coloured; then add three or four green apples in slices, and when these are dissolved, place your pieces of any kind of fish, which you have previously fried in a frying-pan, on the top of the onions, etc., sprinkle a spoonful of curry powder all over the fish, put the lid on the saucepan, and set the whole on the hob of a moderate fire, or in the oven, if you have one, to remain simmering for about half an hour; the curry will then be ready to be eaten with well-boiled rice.

No. 92. THIS IS THE WAY TO BOIL RICE.

I recommend you to buy Patna rice, as it is the cheapest; it is best to soak it in water overnight, as it then requires less time to boil it, and moreover, when soaked, the rice becomes lighter, from the fact that the grains separate more readily while boiling. Put the rice on to boil in plenty of cold water, stirring it from the bottom of the saucepan occasionally while it is boiling fast; when the grains separate at the ends, and thus appear to form the letter X, the rice will be done; it requires about half an hour's gentle boiling. When the rice is done, drain it in a colander, and place it before the fire, stirring it now and then with a fork.

No. 93. RICE DUMPLINGS.

Boil one pound of rice as directed in the foregoing Number, and when thoroughly drained free from excess of moisture, knead the rice with a spoon in a basin into a smooth, compact kind of paste, and use this to cover some peeled apples with in the same way as you would make an ordinary apple dumpling. In order the better to enable you to handle the rice-paste with ease, I recommend that each time previously to shaping one of the dumplings, that you should first dip your clean hands in cold water. Let the dumplings, when finished, be tied up in small cloths, and boiled in plenty of hot water for about three-quarters of an hour. The cloths used for these dumplings must be greased.

D

No. 94. Plum or Currant Dough Pudding.

Ingredients, two pounds of dough from the baker's, four ounces of plums or currants, a pinch of allspice, ditto of salt, a gill of milk. Mix all the above ingredients together in a pan; tie up the pudding in a well-greased pudding-cloth, and place it in a pot containing *boiling* water, and allow it to continue boiling for two hours; at the end of this time the pudding will be done, and may be turned out on its dish.

No. 95. Christmas Plum Pudding.

Ingredients, two pounds of flour, twelve ounces of raisins, twelve ounces of currants, twelve ounces of peeled and chopped apples, one pound of chopped suet, twelve ounces of sugar, four eggs, one pint and a-half of milk or beer, one ounce of salt, half an ounce of ground allspice. Boil the pudding four hours. First, put the flour, suet, and all the fruit in a large pan; mix these well together, and having made a deep hole in the middle thereof with your fist, add the salt, sugar, and allspice, and half a pint of the milk, or beer, to dissolve them; next, add the four eggs, and the remaining pint of milk, or beer; mix all vigorously together with the hand, tie up the pudding in a well-greased and floured cloth, boil it for at least four hours, taking care that the water boils before the pudding is put in the pot to boil. When done, turn the pudding out on its dish, and, if you can afford it, pour over it the following sauce:—

No. 96. Sweet Pudding Sauce.

Ingredients, two ounces of common flour, ditto of butter, ditto of sugar, chopped lemon-peel, half a gill of any kind of spirits, and half a pint of water. First mix the flour, butter, and sugar in a small saucepan by kneading the ingredients well together with a wooden spoon, then add the water, spirits, and lemon-peel; stir the sauce on the fire till it comes to a boil, and then pour it all over the pudding.

No. 97. JAM PUDDING.

Ingredients, one pound of flour, six ounces of suet, half a pint of water, a pinch of salt, one pound of any kind of common jam, at 7d. Mix the flour, suet, water, and salt into a firm, compact kind of paste; roll this out with a rolling-pin, sprinkling some flour on the table to prevent the paste from sticking to either; fold up the paste, and roll it out again; repeat the rolling-out and folding three times; this operation will make the paste lighter. Next, roll out the paste one foot long by eighteen inches wide, spread the jam all over this, roll up the pudding in the form of a bolster, roll it up in a well-greased and floured cloth, tie it up tightly at both ends; put the pudding into a pot of *boiling* water, and boil it for nearly two hours, and when done, turn the pudding out carefully on to its dish, without breaking the crust.

No. 98. RHUBARB PIE.

A bundle of rhubarb, one pound of flour, six ounces of butter, or lard, or dripping, half a pint of water, a pinch of salt, ditto of baking-powder, eight ounces of moist sugar. First, cut up the rhubarb in pieces about an inch long, wash them in plenty of water, and drain them in a colander, or sieve. Next, place the flour in a pan, or on the table, make a hollow in the middle with your fist, place the salt and the baking-powder in it, pour in the water to dissolve them, then add the butter; mix all together by working the ingredients with the fingers of both hands, until the whole has become a firm, smooth, compact kind of paste. You now put the cleaned rhubarb into a pie-dish, with the sugar and a gill of water, roll out the paste to the exact size of the dish, and after wetting the edges of the dish all round, place the rolled-out paste upon it, and by pressing the thumb of the right hand all round the upper part of the edge, the paste will be effectually fastened on, so as to prevent the juice from running out at the sides; a small hole the size of a sixpence must be made at the top of the pie, for ventilation, or otherwise the pie would burst. Bake the pie for an hour and a quarter.

No. 99. Fruit Pies in general.

All kinds of fruit pies are made as shown in the foregoing Number.

No. 100. A Cheap Kind of Mince-meat.

Ingredients, eight ounces of stoned raisins, eight ounces of washed and dried currants, one pound of tripe, one pound of chopped suet, four ounces of shred candied peel, one pound of moist sugar, one ounce of allspice, the juice and the chopped rind of three lemons, half a gill of rum. First chop the raisins, currants, apples, and the tripe all together, or separately, until well mixed; then place these in a pan, add the remainder of the ingredients, mix them thoroughly until well incorporated with each other; put the mince-meat into a clean dry stone jar, tie some thick paper, or a piece of bladder over the top, and keep it in a cool place till wanted for use.

No. 101. Mince-pie Paste.

Ingredients, one pound of flour, eight ounces of butter or lard, three gills of water, half an ounce of salt, a tea-spoonful of baking-powder. Place the flour on the table, hollow out a hole or well in the centre with your fist, place the salt and baking-powder in this, add the water and the butter, work all together lightly with the fingers, without positively absorbing or entirely uniting the butter with the flour, but, on the contrary, keeping the butter in distinct pieces here and there; then roll up the paste in the form of a ball of dough, spread it out on the floured table, and, with a rolling-pin, roll it out to the extent of eighteen inches in length, by eight inches wide; then fold the paste in three equal folds, roll it out the reverse way, fold it up again as before, and after repeating the rolling out and folding up a third time, the paste will be ready for use.

No. 102. To make a Mince Pie.

Having prepared the paste according to the directions given in the foregoing Number, divide it in two equal parts, roll these out either round or square, place one of the flats on a tin baking-dish, wet all round the edge of the paste, spread some of the mincemeat about half an inch thick all over the paste to within an inch of its edge, then cover all in by laying the other flat of paste evenly upon the whole, press all round the edge of the pie with your thumb to secure the mince-meat from running out at the sides, score the pie neatly over the surface, in the form of reversed strokes, and bake it for an hour.

No. 103. Jam Tart.

Prepare some paste, as in No. 101, and use this to make a jam tart, as directed for making a mince-pie, using any kind of common jam, instead of mincemeat, for the purpose.

No. 104. Baked Apple Dumplings.

Ingredients, one pound of flour, four ounces of chopped suet, half a pint of water, a pinch of salt, eight or ten large apples peeled. With the above ingredients prepare some suet paste, as directed in No. 97; divide the paste into about eight equal

parts, roll these with flour into balls, and after having
first rolled them out with a rolling-pin to the size of
a large saucer, envelop an apple in each flat of paste,
by first wetting the edges with water, and then
gathering them round in a purse-like form, and twist-
ing the ends tightly together to fasten them securely.
The dumplings, thus formed, must be placed on the
twisted end, at equal distances of three inches apart
from each other, upon a tin baking-dish, and baked
in the oven for about three-quarters of an hour.

No. 105. PANCAKES FOR SHROVE TUESDAY.

Ingredients, twelve ounces of flour, three eggs,
one pint of milk, a teaspoonful of salt, a little grated
nutmeg, and chopped lemon-peel. First, put the flour
into a basin, hollow out the centre, add the salt, nutmeg, lemon-peel, and a drop of milk, to dissolve them;
then break in the eggs, work all together, with a spoon,
into a smooth soft paste, then add the remainder of
the milk, work the whole vigorously until it forms a
smooth liquid batter. Next, set a frying-pan on the
fire, and, as soon as it gets hot, wipe it out clean with
a cloth, then run about a teaspoonful of lard all over
the bottom of the hot frying-pan, pour in half a small
teacupful of the batter, place the pan over the fire,
and, in about a minute or so, the pancake will have
become set sufficiently firm to enable you to turn it
over in the frying-pan, in order that it may be baked
on the other side also; the pancake done on both
sides, turn it out on its dish, and sprinkle a little
sugar over it: proceed to use up the remaining batter
in the same manner.

No. 106. RAISINET—A PRESERVE FOR WINTER.

Ingredients, twelve pounds of fruit, consisting of
peeled apples, pears, plums, and blackberries, in equal
proportion; six pounds of raw sugar, at $4\frac{1}{2}d$. per

pound; one quart of water. Bake three hours in a slack or slow oven. First, prepare the fruit, and put it in mixed layers of plums, pears, berries, apples, alternating each other, in stone jars. Next, put the six pounds of sugar in a clean saucepan, with the quart of water, and stir it with a spoon on the fire till it comes to a gentle boil; remove the dirty scum from the surface of the sugar; and, after allowing it to boil for ten minutes, pour it in equal proportions into the jar or jars containing the fruits, and place them in a moderate heat to bake slowly for three hours at least. When boiling the sugar for this purpose, remember that it is most prudent to use a saucepan capable of containing double the quantity, as sugar is very liable to boil over and waste. When the fruit is nearly dissolved, the raisinet will be done; it must then be removed to a cool place until it has become thoroughly cold and partially set firm; the jars should then be tied down with thick paper, or bladder, and kept in the cellar for winter use, either for making puddings or tarts, or for spreading on bread for the children.

No. 107. CURRANT JAM.

Ingredients, twelve pounds of picked currants, either red, black, or white, or, if agreeable, mixed; eight pounds of raw sugar, three pints of water. If you could borrow what is called a preserving-pan from a neighbour, it would suit the purpose better than a pot; but, failing the preserving-pan, put the eight pounds of sugar in a four-gallon iron pot, with the three pints of water; stir these on the fire till the sugar boils; remove the scum from the surface, and, when it has boiled for about ten minutes, add the currants, and keep stirring the jam, while it boils for half an hour; and then, if it presents the appearance of being rather thick, and the currants partly dissolved, it will be ready to pour into stone jars, which, after being allowed to cool all night, are to be tied down with paper, and kept in a cold place for winter's use. All kinds of seed fruit can be prepared in the same manner, as well as all kinds of plums.

No. 108. How to Preserve Rhubarb.

Free the rhubarb from leaves, cut it up in inch lengths, wash and drain it in a sieve or colander. Next, put the rhubarb in a sufficiently large pot, or preserving-pan, with a little water—say a pint of water to ten pounds of rhubarb, and put this on the fire, with the lid on, to boil until dissolved to a pulp, stirring it occasionally; and, as soon as all the rhubarb is dissolved, add six pounds of moist sugar, and stir the whole continuously on the fire while boiling fast, until reduced to a rather stiff paste or marmalade—this will require about half an hour's boiling; the preserve or jam must then be immediately put into jars, or gallipots, and, when cold, is to be covered with stiff paper, and tied round with string. Keep the jam in a cold place, for use.

No. 109. How to make Gooseberry Jam.

Pick ten pounds of ripe gooseberries, put them in a covered pot, with a pint of water, and set them on the fire to boil to a pulp, stirring them frequently, and, when they are thoroughly dissolved, add six pounds of sugar, and stir the whole continuously while boiling on the fire, until the jam is reduced to a rather stiff paste; it must then be poured into galli-pots, and, when cold, is to be covered with paper, and tied round with string.

No. 110. Baked Pears.

Put the pears, standing up side by side in rows, with their stalks uppermost, in an earthenware baking dish; add a sprinkle of moist sugar, a few cloves, and a pint of cider or water, and bake them until they are done. The time for cooking them depends upon their size and kind.

No. 111. Baked Apples.

Put the apples on a baking-dish, with a sprinkle of sugar, and a drop of cider or water, and set them in the oven to bake. Baked apples or pears, with bread, form a cheap, wholesome, and proper kind of supper for children.

No. 112. To make Elder Wine.

Ingredients, two gallons of elderberries, two quarts of damsons, eight pounds of raw sugar, at $4\frac{1}{3}d.$ per pound, two gallons of water, two ounces of ginger, one ounce of cloves, and half a pint of fresh yeast. To make this quantity of elder wine, you must have a copper, a tub, a large canvas or loose flannel bag, and a five-gallon barrel. First, crush the elderberries and damsons thoroughly in the pot or copper in which they are to be boiled; then add the water, and keep stirring all together as it boils, until the fruit is well dissolved; and then use a wooden bowl or a basin to pour the whole into a loose flannel bag, steadily fixed across two stout sticks, resting safely on two chairs, or, if you have one, a large coarse sieve instead. When all the liquor has passed through into the tub, put the dregs back into the copper, to be boiled up with a couple of quarts of water, and then to be strained to the other liquor. The next part of the process is to put the whole of the elderberry juice back into the clean pot or copper, with the sugar, and the spice, well bruised with a hammer; stir all together, on the fire, and allow the wine to boil gently for half an hour, and pour the wine into the clean tub to cool; the half-pint of yeast must then be added, and thoroughly mixed by stirring.

At the end of two days, skim off the yeast which, by that time, will have risen to the surface. The elder wine must now be put into the barrel, and kept in the cellar with the bung-hole left open for a fortnight; at the end of this time, a stiff brown paper should be pasted over the bung-hole, and after standing for a month or six weeks, the wine will be ready for use. To be obliged to buy all the ingredients for making elder wine, would render it a matter of great difficulty—perhaps, in some cases, an impossibility; but, remember, that when living in the country, where in some parts elderberries grow in the hedge-rows, you may have them for the trouble of gathering them, in which case the elder wine would be cheaper, and more easily within your means.

No. 113. VEGETABLE PORRIDGE.

Scrape and peel the following vegetables:—six carrots, six turnips, six onions, three heads of celery, and three parsnips; slice up all these very thinly, and put them into a two-gallon pot, with four ounces of butter, a handful of parsley, ditto of chervil, and a good sprig of thyme, and fill up with water or pot liquor, if you happen to have any; season with pepper and salt, and put the whole to boil very gently on the fire for two hours; at the end of this time the vegetables will be done to a pulp, and the whole must be rubbed through a colander with a wooden spoon, and afterwards put back into the pot and stirred over the fire, to make it hot for dinner.

No. 114. PUMPKIN PORRIDGE.

I am aware that pumpkins are not generally grown in this country as an article of food for the poorer classes, and more is the pity, for they require but little trouble to rear, and yield an abundance of nutritious and cooling food, at a small cost; the chief reason for the short supply is, I imagine, the want of knowledge for turning the pumpkin to good account as an article of food. I am now about to supply easy instruction to convey that knowledge to whomsoever may stand in need of it. Peel and slice up as much pumpkin as will produce about eight ounces for each person, and put this into a boiling pot, with two ounces of butter, and a quart of water; set the whole to boil very gently on the fire, until the pumpkin is reduced to a pulp, and then add half-a-pint of buttermilk, or skim milk, to every person who is to partake of the porridge. You then stir the porridge over the fire for about fifteen minutes longer, taking care that it does not boil over; season with salt and a little nutmeg, and eat it with toasted bread for breakfast, or any other meal.

No. 115. RICE-MILK FOR SIX PERSONS.

Put one pound of Patna rice in a boiling pot with two ounces of butter, two quarts of water, a small bit of cinnamon or lemon-peel, and a little salt; put the lid on, and set the rice to boil very gently indeed close to the hob, until the rice is done quite soft; this will take about one hour and a quarter; then add three pints of skim milk, and after having stirred the rice-milk again over the fire for ten minutes longer, it may be sweetened with a little honey or sugar, and will produce an excellent breakfast for at least six persons.

No. 116. KNUCKLE OF VEAL AND RICE.

A small knuckle, or scrag-end of neck of veal, is sometimes to be purchased very cheap; I will therefore suppose that you may, once in a way, provide such a thing, and this is the way you should cook it to the best advantage. Put the knuckle of veal in a boiling pot, with a pound of bacon, two pounds of rice, six onions, three carrots cut in pieces, some peppercorns, and salt in moderation on account of the bacon; add three or four quarts of water, and set the whole to stew very gently over a moderate fire for about three hours. This will produce a good substantial dinner for at least ten persons.

No. 117. IRISH STEW.

Inferior parts of any kind of meat make a good Irish stew. Let the meat be cut in pieces the size of an egg, well rubbed all over with pepper and salt, and placed in a good-sized pot or saucepan; add peeled onions in the proportion of six to the pound of meat, and enough water just to cover in the whole. Next, set the stew on the fire to boil very gently for an hour and a-half, then add such quantity of peeled and split potatoes as you may think will suffice for the number of persons about to dine off the stew, and put the whole back on the fire to boil briskly until the potatoes are thoroughly done soft; the Irish stew will then be ready to eat.

No. 118. FISH SOUP.

Cod-fish cuttings, Dutch plaice, skate, dabs, haddocks, cod's-heads, cod's-tails, or any fresh-water fish you may happen to catch when fishing; conger eels, cut in slices, and almost any kind of fish which may come within reach of your means, are all more or less fit for making a good mess of soup for a meal. First, chop fine some onions, and put them in a pot with enough water to furnish about half a pint for each person to be provided for, and set this on the fire to boil for ten minutes; then add your pieces of fish, of about four ounces each; season with thyme, pepper, and salt, and boil the soup for about fifteen minutes longer, when it will be ready for dinner. Some well-boiled potatoes will prove a welcome addition to this soup.

Note.—This kind of fish soup will prove the more advantageous about or near the sea-coast, where inferior kinds of fish are always very cheap.

No. 119. Soused Mackerel.

When mackerel are to be bought at six for a shilling, this kind of fish forms a cheap dinner. On such occasions, the mackerel must be placed heads and tails in an earthen dish or pan, seasoned with chopped onions, black pepper, a pinch of allspice, and salt; add sufficient vinegar and water in equal proportions to cover the fish. Bake either in your own oven, if you possess one, or else send them to the baker's.

Note.—Herrings, sprats, or any other cheap fish, are soused in the same manner.

No. 120. A Dinner of Red Herrings.

The cheaper sort of red herrings are always too salt, and unpleasantly strong-flavoured, and are therefore an indifferent kind of food, unless due precaution is taken to soak them in water for an hour before they are cooked. First, soak the red herrings in water for an hour; wipe, and split them down the back; toast or broil them on both sides for two or three minutes, and having placed them on a dish, put a bit of butter and some chopped onion upon each herring; pour a little vinegar over all, and this will make a cheap and savoury dish to be eaten with well-boiled potatoes.

No. 121. To Fry Fish.

For this purpose you must have some kind of fat. Either lard, butter, or dripping fat, would be excellent; but they must be bought, and cost a little money. True; but then, if you can afford yourselves a bit of meat occasionally, by dint of good thrift you should save the fat from the boiled meat, or the dripping from your baked meats, and thus furnish yourselves with fat for frying your fish twice a-week; and let me tell you that by introducing fish as an occasional part of your daily food, your health, as well as your pockets, would feel the benefit of such a system of economy. Suppose, then, that you have bought some cheap kind of fish, such as herrings, large flounders, plaice, small soles, or any other small or flat fish. First of all, let the fish be washed and wiped dry, and rubbed all over with a little flour. Next, put about two ounces of fat, free from water, in a frying-pan on the fire, and, as soon as it is hot, put the fish in to fry, one or two at a time, according to their size, as, unless they have room enough in the frying-pan they do not fry well; this must be carefully attended to, and when the fish is a little browned on one side, turn it over with a tin fish-slice, that it may be fried on the other side also; and, as soon as done, place the fried fish on a dish and then fry the others. When all your fish are fried, with what fat remains in the pan fry some onions, and place them round the fish, and, by way of adding an extra relish to your meal, just throw a few table-spoonfuls of vinegar, some pepper and salt, into the frying-pan, give it a boil up, and pour this round the fish.

No. 122. SALT FISH WITH PARSNIPS.

Salt fish must always be well soaked in plenty of cold water the whole of the night before it is required for the following day's dinner. The salt fish must be put on to boil in plenty of cold water, without any salt, and when thoroughly done, should be well-drained free from any water, and placed on a dish with plenty of well-boiled parsnips. Some sauce may be poured over the fish, which is to be made as follows : viz.—Mix two ounces of butter with three ounces of flour, pepper and salt, a small glassful of vinegar, and a good half-pint of water. Stir this on the fire till it boils. A few hard-boiled eggs, chopped up and mixed in this sauce, would render the dish more acceptable.

No. 123. Baked Fish.

Wash and wipe the fish, and lay it, heads and tails, in a baking-dish, the bottom of which has been spread all over with a little butter or dripping, add a little vinegar and water, and, when procurable, some mushroom ketchup. Season with chopped onions and parsley, shake plenty of raspings of bread all over the top of the fish, and bake it in your oven, or else send it to the baker's.

No. 124. Baked Cod's Head.

First, make some stuffing with one pound of bruised crumb of bread, mixed with six ounces of chopped suet, two eggs, chopped parsley, onions and thyme, and seasoned with pepper and salt. Put this stuffing inside the cod's head, and place it in a baking-dish with two ounces of butter, a gill of vinegar, and a pint and a half of water. Spread a little of the butter all over the cod's head, and then a thick coating of bread-raspings all over it ; bake it for an hour in the oven. A few oysters would be an improvement.

No. 125. Bouillabaisse Soup.

Put the following ingredients in a saucepan to boil on the fire :—four onions and six tomatoes, or red love-apples, cut in thin slices, some thyme and winter savory, a little salad-oil, a wine-glassful of vinegar, pepper and salt, and a pint of water to each person. When the soup has boiled fifteen minutes, throw in your fish, cut in pieces or slices, and, as soon as the fish is done, eat the soup with some crusts of bread or toast in it. All kinds of fish suit this purpose.

No. 126. To Boil Fish.

Put the fish on in sufficient water to cover it, add a small handful of salt, and, providing that the fish is not larger than mackerel, soles, or whiting, it will be cooked by the time that the water boils. Yet it is always best to try whether it requires to boil a little longer, as underdone fish is unwholesome. Boiled fish requires some kind of sauce. Try the following, viz:—

No. 127. Parsley Sauce.

Chop a handful of parsley and mix it in a stew-pan with two ounces of butter, two ounces of flour, pepper and salt; moisten with half a pint of water and a table-spoonful of vinegar. Stir the parsley-sauce on the fire till it boils, and then pour it over the fish, drained free from water, on its dish.

No. 128. Anchovy Sauce.

Mix two ounces of butter with two ounces of flour, in a saucepan. Add a spoonful of essence of anchovy, and half a pint of water. Stir the sauce on the fire till it boils.

No. 129. Baked Skate.

Chop three onions, and fry them of a light-brown colour in two ounces of butter, then add half a pint of vinegar, pepper and salt, and allow the whole to boil on the fire for five minutes. Put the skate in a baking dish, pour the sauce over it, and also just enough water to reach to its surface. Strew a thick coating of bread-raspings on the fish, and bake it for an hour and a half at rather moderate heat.

No. 130. How to Brew your own Beer.

The first preparatory step towards brewing is to gather your necessary plant together in proper working order, and thoroughly clean. Your plant or utensils must consist of the following articles, viz. :— A thirty-gallon copper, two cooling-tubs capable of holding each about thirty gallons ; a mash-tub of sufficient size to contain fifty-four gallons, and another tub of smaller size, called an underback ; a bucket or pail, a wooden hand-bowl, a large wooden funnel, a mash-stirrer, four scraped long stout sticks, a good-sized loose-wrought wicker basket for straining the beer, and another small bowl-shaped wicker basket, called a tapwaist, to fasten inside the mash-tub on to the inner end of the spigot and faucet, to keep back the grains when the wort is being run off out of the mash-tub. You will also require some beer barrels, a couple of brass or metal cocks, some vent-pegs, and some bungs. I do not pretend to assert that the whole of the foregoing articles are positively indispensable for brewing your own beer. I merely enumerate what is most proper to be used ; leaving the manner and means of replacing such of these articles as may be out of your reach very much to your intelligence in contriving to use such as you possess, or can borrow from a neighbour, instead. Spring water, from its hardness, is unfit for brewing ; fresh fallen rain water, caught in clean tubs, or water fetched from a brook or river, are best adapted for brewing ; as, from the fact of their being free from all calcareous admixture, their consequent softness gives them the greater power to extract all the goodness and strength from the malt and hops.

In order to ensure having good wholesome beer, it is necessary to calculate your brewing at the rate of two bushels of malt and two pounds of hops to

E

fifty-four gallons of water; these proportions, well managed, will produce three kilderkins of good beer. I recommend that you should use malt and hops of the best quality only; as their plentiful yield of beneficial substance fully compensates for their somewhat higher price. A thin shell, well filled up plump with the interior flour, and easily bitten asunder, is a sure test of good quality in malt; superior hops are known by their light greenish-yellow tinge of colour, and also by their bright, dry, yet somewhat gummy feel to the touch, without their having any tendency to clamminess. The day before brewing, let all your tackle be well scrubbed and rinsed clean, the copper wiped out, and all your tubs and barrels half filled with cold water, to soak for a few hours, so as to guard against any chance of leakage, and afterwards emptied, and set to dry in the open air, weather permitting; or otherwise, before the fire. Fasten the tapwaist inside the mash-tub to the inner end of the faucet and spigot, taking care to place the mash-tub in an elevated position, resting upon two benches or stools. Early in the dawn of morning, light the fire under your copper, filled with water overnight, and, as soon as it boils, with it fill the mash-tub rather more than three-parts full; and as soon as the first heat of the water has subsided, and you find that you are able to bear your fingers drawn slowly through it without experiencing pain, you must then throw in the malt, stirring it about for ten minutes or so; then lay some sticks across the mash-tub, and cover it with sacks or blankets, and allow it to steep for three hours. At the end of the three hours, let off the wort from the mash-tub into the underback-tub, which has been previously placed under the spigot and faucet ready to receive it; pouring the first that runs out back into the mash, until the wort runs free from grains, etc.; now put the hops into the underback-

tub, and let the wort run out upon them. Your copper having been refilled, and boiled again while the mash is in progress, you must now pour sufficient boiling water into the grains left in the mash-tub to make up your quantity of fifty-four gallons; and when this second mashing shall have also stood some two hours, let it be drawn off, and afterwards mixed with the first batch of wort, and boil the whole at two separate boilings, with the hops equally divided; each lot to be allowed to boil for an hour and a-half after it has commenced boiling. The beer is now to be strained through the loose wicker basket into your cooling tubs and pans; the more you have of these the better the beer, from its cooling quickly. And when the beer has cooled to the degree of water which has stood in the house in summer-time for some hours, let it all be poured into your two or three largest tubs, keeping back a couple or three quarts in a pan, with which to mix a pint of good yeast and a table-spoonful of common salt; stir this mixture well together, keep it in rather a warm part of the house, and in the course of half an hour or so, it will work up to the top of the basin or pan. This worked beer must now be equally divided between the two or three tubs containing the bulk of the beer, and is to be well mixed in by ladling it about with a wooden hand-bowl for a couple of minutes. This done, cover over the beer with sacks or blankets stretched upon sticks across the tubs, and leave them in this state for forty-eight hours. The next thing to be seen to is to get your barrels placed in proper order and position for being filled; and to this end attend strictly to the following directions, viz. :—
First, skim off the scum, which is yeast, from the top or surface of the tubs, and next, draw off the beer through the spigot, and with the wooden funnel placed in the bung-hole, proceed to fill up the barrels

not quite full; and, remember, that if a few hops are put into each before filling in the beer, it will keep all the better. Reserve some of the beer with which to fill up the barrels as they throw up the yeast while the beer is working; and when the yeast begins to fall, lay the bungs upon the bung-holes, and at the end of ten days or a fortnight, hammer the bungs in tight, and keep the vent-pegs tight also. In about two months' time after the beer has been brewed, it will be in a fit condition for drinking.

No. 131. How to Bake your own Bread.

Put a bushel of flour into a trough, or a large pan; with your fist make a deep hole in the centre thereof; put a pint of good fresh yeast into this hollow; add thereto two quarts of warm water, and work in with these as much of the flour as will serve to make a soft smooth kind of batter. Strew this over with just enough flour to hide it; then cover up the trough with its lid, or with a blanket to keep all warm, and when the leaven has risen sufficiently to cause the flour to crack all over its surface, throw in a handful of salt, work all together; add just enough lukewarm soft water to enable you to work the whole into a firm, compact dough, and after having kneaded this with your fists until it becomes stiff and comparatively tough, shake a little flour over it, and again cover it in with a blanket to keep it warm, in order to assist its fermentation. If properly managed, the fermentation will be accomplished in rather less than half an hour. Meanwhile that the bread is being thus far prepared, you will have heated your oven to a satisfactory degree of heat, with a sufficient quantity of dry, small wood faggots; and when all the wood is burnt, sweep out the oven clean and free from all ashes. Divide your dough into four-pound loaves, knead them into round shapes, making a hole at the top with your thumb, and immediately put them out of hand into the oven to bake, closing the oven-door upon them. In about two hours' time they will be thoroughly baked, and are then to be taken out of the oven, and allowed to become quite cold before they are put away in the cupboard.

No. 132. YORKSHIRE PIE-CLATES FOR TEA.

Ingredients, one pound of flour, two ounces of grocer's currants, three gills of milk, and a pinch of baking-powder. Mix the above ingredients together in a pan into a firm, smooth, compact paste. Divide this into eight equal parts, roll each into a ball with flour, then roll them out with a rolling-pin, with a little flour shaken on the table to prevent the paste from sticking, to the size of a tea-saucer, and bake the pie-clates upon a griddle-iron fixed over a clear fire to the upper bar of the grate. In about two or three minutes' time they will be done on the under-side; they must then be turned over that they may be also baked on the other side, and then taken off the griddle-iron, placed on a plate, and a little butter spread upon each as they are done out of hand.

No. 133. HARD BISCUITS.

Ingredients, one pound of flour, half a pint of hot milk, a tea-spoonful of salt, a pinch of baking-powder; bake them a quarter of an hour. Mix the above ingredients into a firm paste, well kneaded until it becomes quite tough; then let the paste rest covered over with a cloth for half an hour, after which it is to be divided into eight equal parts, rolled out to the size of tea-saucers, placed upon baking-tins, pricked all over with a fork, and baked in a brisk oven for about fifteen minutes.

No. 134. GINGERBREAD NUTS.

Ingredients, one pound of flour, half a pint of treacle, two ounces of butter, half an ounce of ground ginger, a pinch of allspice, a tea-spoonful of carbonate of soda, and a pinch of salt. Mix all the above ingredients into a firm, well-kneaded stiff paste, divide this into about twenty-four round balls rolled into shape like walnuts, place these upon greased baking-tins at distances of two inches apart from each other, and bake the gingerbread nuts in a rather brisk oven for about fifteen minutes.

No. 135. HOW TO STEAM POTATOES.

Peel the potatoes thinly, wash them clean, put them in the steamer, over *boiling* water, which must be kept briskly boiling until the potatoes are thoroughly done, the length of time depending very much on their size. I am aware that it is not in the power of all to possess a potato-steamer, although one may be purchased at Adams & Son's, in the Haymarket, for a few shillings; and therefore I will give you instructions how to boil potatoes.

No. 136. HOW TO BOIL POTATOES.

Wash the potatoes clean, and put them on to boil in a saucepan, with cold water just enough to cover them; place the saucepan on the hob, close to the fire, and allow them to remain in that position for a quarter of an hour, by which time the water will have gradually reached to the boiling point; the saucepan should now be allowed to boil until the potatoes are done through, and then pour off the water; put the lid on again with a cloth on the top, place the saucepan close to the fire for about five minutes, and when you turn them out on their dish you will find that you have a well-boiled, mealy potato before you.

No. 137. Baked or Roasted Potatoes.

You do not require that I should tell you that when you have no oven you can easily roast your potatoes by placing them on the hobs, bars, and under the fire-grate; and if you are attentive to their being well roasted, by turning them about now and then, so that they may be done all over alike, you need not be deprived of a baked potato for the want of an oven. When the potatoes are roasted, slightly squeeze each separately in a cloth, to make them mealy, then split them open; season them with a bit of butter, or dripping, a little bit of chopped shalot, pepper, and salt, and this will afford you a nice relish for supper.

No. 138. How to Fry Potatoes.

Peel, split, and cut the potatoes into slices of *equal* thickness, say the thickness of two penny pieces; and as they are cut out of hand, let them be dropped into a pan of cold water. When about to fry the potatoes, first drain them on a clean cloth, and dab them all over, in order to absorb all moisture; while this has been going on, you will have made some kind of fat (entirely free from water or gravy, such as lard, for instance) very hot in a frying-pan, and into this drop your prepared potatoes, only a good handful at a time; as, if you attempt to fry too many at once, instead of being crisp, as they should be, the potatoes will fry flabby, and consequently will be unappetising. As soon as the first lot is fried in a satisfactory manner, drain them from the fat with a skimmer, or spoon, and then fry the remainder; and when all are fried, shake a little salt over them.

No. 139. How to Fry Potatoes an easier Way.

When it happens that by some chance or other you have some cold boiled potatoes, this is the way to

fry them:—First cut the potatoes in thick slices, and
fry them in a frying-pan with butter or dripping, just
enough to season them, and as they fry, lift or scrape
them from the bottom of the pan with an iron spoon,
to prevent them from sticking to the bottom and
burning, which, by imparting a bitter taste, would
spoil them; when all are fried of a very light brown
colour, season with pepper and salt.

No. 140. How to Mash Potatoes.

Either steam or boil the potatoes, as indicated in
Nos. 135 and 136, and immediately after they are
done, while steaming hot, put the potatoes into a clean
saucepan, and break or mash them by stirring them
vigorously with a fork; when all are broken smooth
and mealy, add a little *hot* milk, with a bit of butter,
pepper, and salt; work the whole well together for a
few minutes, and eat the mashed potatoes while hot.

No. 141. Baked Mashed Potatoes.

Prepare the mashed potatoes as shown in the preceding Number, put them in a dish, smooth them over
with a knife, put some bits of butter on the top, and
set them before the fire, turning them occasionally to
brown them equally all round.

No. 142. Mashed Potatoes with Ling.

Ling is a kind of dried salt fish; it is cheaper
than the ordinary sort of salted codfish. It should be
washed and well soaked in plenty of tepid water for six
hours before it is boiled in cold water, and when it
has been taken out, should be divided into large flakes,
mixed with mashed potatoes, and baked in a dish, as
directed in the preceding Number.

No. 143. How to Stew Potatoes.

First boil the potatoes, and then put a little

butter, a chopped onion, half a pint of milk, or water, pepper and salt to season; boil this for ten minutes, then add the potatoes, previously cooked; boil all together for ten minutes, and dish them up.

No. 144. BUTTERED PARSNIPS.

Scrape or peel the parsnips, and boil them in hot water till they are done quite tender, then drain off all the water, add a bit of butter, some chopped parsley, pepper and salt; shake them together on the fire until all is well mixed.

No. 145. BUTTERED SWEDISH TURNIPS.

Swedish turnips are mostly given as food to cattle; true, but there is no good reason why they should not be considered as excellent food for Christians, for they are sweeter, and yield more substance than the ordinary turnips; let them be peeled, boiled in plenty of water, and when done, mashed with a little milk, butter, pepper, and salt.

No. 146. HOW TO COOK SPINACH.

Pick it thoroughly, wash the spinach, boil it in plenty of hot water with salt in it, and when it is done, drain it free from all moisture, chop it up, put it in a saucepan with butter, pepper, and salt; stir all together on the fire for five minutes.

No. 147. FRIED CABBAGE AND BACON.

First, boil the cabbage, and when done and drained free from water, chop it up. Next fry some rashers of bacon, and when done, lay them on a plate before the fire; put the chopped cabbage in the frying-pan, and fry it with the fat from the bacon, then put this on a dish with the rashers upon it.

No. 148. PEAS AND BACON.

Shave off any brown rancid part from the bacon, and put it on to boil in plenty of cold water; when it is nearly done put in the peas with a good bunch of mint, and let all boil together until the peas are done soft; then dish up the peas round the bacon.

No. 149. BAKED OR ROASTED ONIONS.

Do not peel the onions, but put them in their natural state to roast on the hobs, turning them round to the fire occasionally, in order that they may be equally roasted all over and through; and when they are well done, remove the outer skin, split them open, add a bit of butter, pepper and salt, and a few drops of vinegar.

No. 150. HOW TO COOK BROAD BEANS.

Boil the beans in hot water with a bunch of winter savory and some salt, and when done and drained, put them in a saucepan with the chopped savory, butter, a pinch of flour, pepper and salt, and toss all together for a few minutes over the fire.

No. 151. HOW TO COOK FRENCH BEANS.

String the beans and boil them in hot water with salt, and when done and drained, put them in a saucepan, with butter, a pinch of flour, chopped parsley, pepper and salt, and stir them gently on the fire for two or three minutes.

No. 152. HOW TO COOK VEGETABLE MARROW.

This is a cheap and excellent vegetable; let them be peeled, split them, and remove the seedy part; boil them in hot water with salt, and when done, eat them with a bit of butter, pepper, and salt.

No. 153. White Haricot Beans.

In France, haricot beans form a principal part in the staple articles of food for the working-classes, and indeed for the entire population; it is much to be desired that some effectual means should be had recourse to for the purpose of introducing and encouraging the use of this most excellent vegetable among the people as a general article of their daily food, more especially in the winter season. If this desideratum could be accomplished, its beneficial result would go far to assist in rendering us in a measure independent of the potato crop, which, of late years, has proved so uncertain. I am aware that haricot beans, as well as lentils, as at present imported and retailed as a mere luxury to such as possess cooks who know how to dress them, might lead to the rejection of my proposal that they should, or could, be adopted as food by the people; but I see no reason why haricot beans should not be imported to this country in such quantities as would enable the importers to retail them at a somewhat similar low price as that in which they are sold at in France. In that case, they would become cheap enough to come within the reach of the poorest. And under the impression that this wish of mine may be eventually realized, I will here give you instructions how to cook haricot beans to the greatest advantage.

No. 154. How to Dress Haricot Beans.

Put a quart of white haricot beans in plenty of cold water in a pan in order that they may soak through the night; the next day drain off the water in which they have soaked, and put them in a pot with three quarts of *cold* water, a little grease or butter, some pepper and salt, and set them on the fire to boil *very gently* until they are thoroughly done; this will take about two hours' gentle boiling: when done, the hari-

cot beans are to be drained free from excess of moisture, and put into a saucepan with chopped parsley,
butter, pepper and salt; stir the whole carefully on the
fire for five minutes, and serve them for dinner with
or without meat as may best suit your means.

No. 155. HARICOT BEANS, ANOTHER WAY.

When the haricot beans have been boiled as shown
in the preceding Number, chop fine a couple of onions,
and fry them in a saucepan with a bit of butter, then
add the haricot beans, pepper and salt; stir all together
and serve them out to your family.

No. 156. A SALAD OF HARICOT BEANS.

Well-boiled haricot beans, cold, are made into an
excellent salad, as follows:—Put the haricot beans
into a bowl, season with chopped parsley, green onions,
salad oil, vinegar, pepper and salt, and slices of beet-
root.   Mix thoroughly.

No. 157. LENTILS.

Lentils are a species of vetches much in use in
France as a staple article of food in the winter; there
are two sorts, those denominated "*à la reine*," a
small brown flat-looking seed, while the other sort is
somewhat larger—of the size of small peas, and flat;
both sorts are equally nutritious, and are to be treated
in exactly the same way as herein indicated for cooking haricot beans.

These, as well as haricot beans, may be boiled
with a piece of bacon.

No. 158. A RELISH FOR SUPPER.

Prepare some oysters, as shown in No. 54, and
when poured upon the toast in their dish, strew all
over their surface equal quantities of bread raspings
and grated cheese; hold a red-hot shovel over the top

until it becomes slightly coloured, and eat this little delicacy while hot.

No. 159. How to Make an Omelet.

Break three or four eggs into a basin, add a little chopped shalot, and parsley, pepper, and salt; put an ounce of butter in a frying-pan on the fire, and as soon as the butter begins to fry, beat up the eggs, etc., with a fork for two minutes; immediately pour the whole into the frying-pan, and put it on the fire, stirring the eggs with an iron spoon as they become set and the omelet appears nearly done; fold all together in the form of a bolster, and turn it out on to its dish.

No. 160. Fried Eggs and Bacon.

First, fry the rashers of bacon, and then break the eggs into the frying-pan without disturbing the yolks, and as soon as these are just set, or half-done, slip them out on to the rashers of bacon which you have already placed in a dish.

No. 161. Buttered Eggs.

Fry half an ounce of butter in a frying-pan, then break three or four eggs into this; season with chopped parsley, pepper and salt, and again set the pan on the fire for two minutes. At the end of this time the eggs will be sufficiently set to enable you to slip them gently out of the pan upon a plate; and to finish cooking the eggs, it will be necessary to place them or hold them in front of the fire for a couple of minutes longer.

No. 162. Eggs with Brown Butter.

Cook the eggs as directed in the foregoing number, and when you have slipped them out on to a dish, put piece of butter into the frying-pan, and stir it on the fire until it becomes quite brown (*not burnt*); then add two table-spoonfuls of vinegar, pepper, and salt; boil for two minutes, and pour this over the eggs.

No. 163. Eggs Stewed with Cheese.

Fry three eggs in a pan with one ounce of butter, seasoned with pepper and salt, and when the eggs are just set firm at the bottom of the pan, slip them off on to a dish, cover them all over with some very thin slices of cheese, set the dish before the fire to melt the cheese, and then eat this cheap little tit-bit with some toast.

No. 164. How to Make a Welsh Rarebit.

First, make a round of hot toast, butter it, and cover it with thin slices of cheese; put it before the fire until the cheese is melted, then season with mustard, pepper, and salt, and eat the rarebit while hot.

No. 165. Egg-hot.

Put a pint of beer on the fire to warm, break an egg into a jug, add a table-spoonful of sugar and some grated nutmeg or ginger; beat all together with a fork for three minutes; then add a drop of the beer, stir well together, and pour the remainder of the hot beer to this, and continue pouring the egg-hot out of the warming-pot into the jug for two minutes, when it will be well mixed and ready to drink.

No. 166. Ginger-pop.

Put a *very clean* pot containing a gallon of water to boil on the fire, and as soon as it begins to boil, add twelve ounces of brown sugar, and one ounce of bruised ginger, and two ounces of cream of tartar;

stir well together; pour the whole into an earthen pan, and cover it over with a cloth, and let the mash remain in this state until it has become quite cold; then stir in half a gill of fresh yeast; stir all well together until thoroughly mixed, cover the pan over with a cloth, and leave the ginger-beer in a cool place to work up; this will take from six to eight hours; the scum which has risen to the top must then be carefully removed with a spoon without disturbing the brightness of the beer, and it is then to be carefully poured off bright into a jug with a spout, to enable you easily to pour it into the bottles. These must be immediately corked down tight, tied across the corks with string, and put away, lying down in the cellar. The ginger-pop will be fit to drink in about four days after it has been bottled.

No. 167. PLUM BROTH.

Boil one quart of any kind of red plums in three pints of water with a piece of cinnamon and four ounces of brown sugar until the plums are entirely dissolved; then rub the whole through a sieve or colander, and give it to the children to eat with bread.

No. 168. PLUM PORRIDGE, COLD.

Boil a quart of red plums in a pint of water, with a bit of cinnamon and four ounces of sugar, until dissolved to a pulp; then rub the whole through a sieve or colander into a large basin, and when this is quite cold, mix in with it about a quart of good milk, and give it to the children to eat with bread for either breakfast or supper.

No. 169. STEWED PRUNES OR PRUENS.

Purchase the cheaper kind of small prunes sold at 4d. per lb.; put them in a saucepan with a pint of water, a bit of lemon-peel, and two ounces of sugar, and allow them to simmer and stew very gently for about half an hour, and then let them become nearly cold. Boil some rice in a cloth, as directed in No. 92, and when done and turned out on its dish, pour the prunes over it for the children's dinner. Once in a way, this cheap and wholesome meal would prove a great treat.

No. 170. A Summer Salad.

Rinse and well shake off all moisture from a couple of cos lettuce, cut them up into a bowl or basin, add a few roughly-chopped green onions, half a gill of cream, a table-spoonful of vinegar, pepper and salt to taste. Mix all together.

No. 171. A Bacon Salad.

Having prepared any kind of salad you may happen to have, such as endive, corn salad, lettuce, celery, mustard and cress, seasoned with beet-root, onions, or shalot; let the salad be cut up into a bowl or basin ready for seasoning in the following manner: —Cut eight ounces of fat bacon into small square pieces the size of a cob-nut, fry these in a frying-pan, and as soon as they are done, pour the whole upon the salad; add two table-spoonfuls of vinegar, pepper and salt to taste. Mix thoroughly.

No. 172. A Plain Salad.

Cos lettuce cut up in a bowl or basin, seasoned with chopped green mint and green onions, a spoonful of moist sugar, vinegar, pepper and salt. Mix thoroughly.

No. 173. Celery Crab Salad.

First thoroughly wash and wipe clean, and then cut a stick of celery into a basin; add two ounces of any kind of cheese sliced very thinly, season with a good tea spoonful of made mustard, a table-spoonful of salad oil, ditto of vinegar, with pepper and salt. Mix thoroughly.

No. 174. How to Mix Mustard.

Put half an ounce of mustard into a teacup, or a small basin, add a little salt; mix thoroughly with just enough boiling water to work the whole into a smooth compact soft paste.

COOKERY AND DIET FOR THE SICK ROOM.

No. 175. Beef Tea.

Chop up a pound of lean beef, and put it on to boil in a saucepan with a quart of water, stirring it on the fire occasionally while it boils rather fast, for at least half an hour; at the end of this time the beef tea will have become reduced to a pint; season with salt to taste, strain it through a clean bit of muslin or rag, and give a tea-cupful of it with dry toast to the patient.

No. 176. Mutton Broth.

Chop a pound of scrag end of neck of mutton into small pieces, and put it into a saucepan, with two ounces of barley, and rather better than a quart of water; set the broth to boil gently on the fire, skim it well, season with a little salt, thyme, parsley, and a couple of turnips; the whole to continue gently boiling on the side of the hob for an hour and a-half; and at the end of this time serve some of the broth strained through a clean rag into a basin; or, if the patient is allowed it, serve the broth with some of the barley and pieces of the meat in it.

F

No. 177. Chicken Broth.

Draw, singe, and cut a chicken into four quarters; wash these, put them into a clean saucepan with a quart of water, and set the broth to boil on the fire; skim it well, season with two ounces of sago, a small sprig of thyme and parsley, and a little salt. Allow the broth to boil very gently for an hour, and then serve some of it with the sago in a cup, and, if allowed, give the patient the chicken separately.

No. 178. A Cheaper Kind of Chicken Broth.

In large towns it is easy to purchase sixpenny-worth of fowls' necks, gizzards, and feet, which, prepared as indicated in the foregoing Number, make excellent broth at a fourth part of the cost occasioned by using a fowl for the same purpose.

No. 179. Veal and Rice Broth.

Cut up one pound and a-half of knuckle of veal, and put it on to boil in a saucepan with a quart of water, four ounces of rice, a small sprig of thyme, and a little parsley; season with a few peppercorns and a little salt; boil very gently for two hours.

No.. 180. Meat Panada for Invalids and Infants.

First, roast whatever kind of meat is intended to be made into panada, and, while it is yet hot, chop up all the lean thereof as fine as possible, and put this with all the gravy that has run from the meat on the plate into a small saucepan with an equal quantity of crumb of bread previously soaked in hot water; season with a little salt (and, if allowed, pepper), stir all together on the fire for ten minutes, and give it in small quantities at a time. This kind of meat panada is well adapted as a nutritious and easily-digested kind of food for old people who have lost the power of mastication, and also for very young children.

No. 181. How to prepare Sago for Invalids.

Put a large table-spoonful of sago into a small saucepan with half a pint of hot water, four lumps of sugar, and, if possible, a small glass of port wine; stir the whole on the fire for a quarter of an hour, and serve it in a teacup.

No. 182. How to prepare Tapioca.

This may be prepared in the same manner as sago; it may also be boiled in beef tea, mutton broth, or chicken broth, and should be stirred while boiling.

Arrow-root is to be prepared exactly after the directions given for the preparation of sago and tapioca.

No. 183. How to make Gruel.

Mix a table-spoonful of Robinson's prepared groats or grits with a tea-cupful of cold water, pour this into a saucepan containing a pint of hot water, and stir it on the fire while it boils for ten minutes; strain the gruel through a sieve or colander into a basin, sweeten to taste, add a spoonful of any kind of spirits, or else season the gruel with salt and a bit of butter.

No. 184. Brown and Polson Gruel.

Brown and Polson's excellent preparation of Indian corn is to be purchased of all grocers throughout the kingdom. Mix a dessert-spoonful of the prepared Indian corn with a wine-glassful of cold water, and pour this into a small saucepan containing half a pint of hot water; stir on the fire for ten minutes, sweeten with moist sugar, flavour with nutmeg or a spoonful of spirits.

No. 185. Gruel made with Oatmeal.

In the absence of groats, oatmeal furnishes the means of making excellent gruel. Mix two table-spoonfuls of oatmeal with a gill of cold water; pour this into a saucepan containing a pint of hot water, stir the gruel on the fire while it boils very gently for about a quarter of an hour, then sweeten with moist sugar, or, if preferred, the gruel may be eaten with a little salt and a bit of butter.

No. 186. How to make Caudle.

Mix four ounces of prepared groats or oatmeal with half a pint of cold ale in a basin, pour this into a saucepan containing a quart of boiling ale, or beer, add a few whole allspice, and a little cinnamon, stir the caudle on the fire for about half an hour, and then strain it into a basin or jug; add a glass of any kind of spirits, and sugar to taste.

No. 187. Rice Gruel, a Remedy for Relaxed Bowels.

Boil very gently eight ounces of rice in a quart of water for about an hour in a saucepan covered with its lid, and placed on the side of the hob; the rice must be so thoroughly done as to present the appear-ance of the grains being entirely dissolved; a bit of orange-peel or cinnamon should be boiled with the rice, and when quite soft, the gruel is to be sweetened with loaf sugar, and a table-spoonful of brandy added.

No 188. How to prepare Arrow-root.

Mix a piled-up dessert-spoonful of arrow-root with half a gill of cold water, and pour this into a small saucepan containing nearly half a pint of boiling water, four lumps of sugar, and a glass of wine; stir the arrow-root while it is boiling on the fire for a few minutes, and then give it to the patient.

Observe that it is essential to perfection in the preparation of arrow-root, and, indeed, of all farinaceous kinds of food, that the whole of the ingredients used in the preparation should be boiled together.

No. 189. How to make Gruel with Pearl Barley.

Put four ounces of pearl barley in a saucepan with two quarts of cold water and a small stick of cinnamon, and set the whole to boil very gently by the side of the fire (partly covered with the lid) for two hours; then add the sugar and the wine, boil all together a few minutes longer, and then strain the gruel through a colander into a jug, to be kept in a cool place until required for use; when it can be warmed up in small quantities.

As this kind of gruel is a powerful cordial, it is to be borne in mind that it should never be administered unless ordered by a medical man.

No. 190. Cow-heel Broth.

Put a cow-heel into a saucepan with three quarts of water, and set it to boil on the fire; skim it well, season with a few peppercorns, a sprig of thyme and parsley, and a dessert-spoonful of salt; boil gently for two hours; at the end of this time the broth will be reduced to half its original quantity; skim off all the grease, and serve the broth with the glutinous part of the heel in it. This kind of broth is both strengthening and healing to the stomach.

No. 191. How to make Calf's-feet Jelly.

Boil two calf's feet in two quarts of water very gently for at least two hours; at the end of this time the liquid will be boiled down to one half of its original quantity; it is then to be strained into a pan, and left to cool till the next day. Scrape and wash off all grease, dab a clean cloth all over the surface to absorb any remaining grease, put the calf's-foot stock or broth into a very clean saucepan, add three ounces of lump sugar, a bit of lemon-peel, the juice of a lemon, a little bruised cinnamon, and half a pint of white wine; boil all together for ten minutes, skim, strain through a doubled piece of muslin into a basin; set the jelly in a very cold place to cool and become firm.

No. 192. How to make Iceland-moss Jelly.

Iceland moss is to be had of all chemists. Put four ounces of Iceland moss to boil in one quart of water, stirring it the whole time it is on the fire; and when it has boiled about three-quarters of an hour, add two ounces of lump sugar and a glass of white wine; strain the jelly through a piece of muslin into a basin, and when it is set firm and cold, let it be given to the patient. This kind of jelly is most beneficial in cases of severe colds, catarrhs, and all pulmonary diseases of the lungs and chest.

No. 193. How to make Blancmange.

Scald, skin, wash, and thoroughly bruise one ounce of sweet almonds with a rolling-pin on a table; put this into a basin with one ounce of lump sugar, and three gills of cold water, and allow the whole to stand and steep for three hours. Next, boil one ounce of shred isinglass, or gelatine, in a gill of water, by stirring it on the fire, while boiling, for ten minutes; pour this to the milk of almonds; strain all through a muslin into a basin, and when the blancmange has become stiff and cold, let it be given to the patient in cases of fevers, or extreme delicacy.

No. 194. How to make Sick-diet Jelly.

Take of sago, tapioca, eringo root, and hartshorn shavings, of each one ounce; and boil the whole in three pints of water until reduced to one pint, stirring all the time; then strain the jelly through a muslin into a basin, and set it aside to become cold. A table-spoonful of this jelly may be given at a time, mixed in broth, milk, chocolate, cocoa, or tea. It is considered to be very strengthening.

No. 195. How to Prepare Isinglass Jelly.

Put one ounce and a-half of isinglass, with two ounces of lump sugar and half a pint of water, into a small stewpan, and stir the whole on the fire while it boils gently for ten minutes; then remove the jelly from the fire, add the juice of three oranges, and the thin pared rind of one orange; stir well together for five minutes, strain through a muslin into a basin, and set the jelly in a cold place to become stiff.

No. 196. How to make Ground-rice Milk.

Put a pint of milk with a bit of cinnamon to boil, mix a large table-spoonful of ground rice quite smooth with a tea-cupful of milk, pour this into the boiling milk, stirring quickly all the time in order to render it smooth; add sugar to sweeten, and stir the ground-rice milk on the fire while boiling for ten minutes. Remember, that whenever you are stirring any kind of sauce, gruel, porridge, or thick milk, etc., on the fire, it is most essential that you should bear with some weight on the edge of the bowl of the spoon to prevent whatever is being stirred from burning at the bottom of the saucepan, as such an accident would infallibly spoil the gruel, etc.

No. 197. How to make a Small Batter-pudding.

Beat up in a basin an egg with a large table-spoonful of flour, and a grain of salt; add, by degrees, a tea-cupful of milk, working all together vigorously; pour this batter into a ready greased inside of a tea-cup, just large enough to hold it; sprinkle a little flour on the top, place a small square clean rag on it, and then, with the spread-out fingers of the right hand, catch up both cloth and tea-cup, holding them up in order to enable you to gather up the ends of the rag tight in your left hand, while with a piece of string held in the right hand, you tie up the pudding securely, and put it on to boil, in boiling water, for a good half-hour; at the end of this time the pudding will be done, and should be eaten immediately with sugar, and a few drops of wine, if allowed and procurable.

No. 198. How to make a Tea-cup Bread-pudding.

Bruise a piece of stale crumb of bread the size of an egg, in a basin, add four lumps of sugar and a very little grated nutmeg, pour half a gill of boiling milk upon these, stir all well together until the sugar is melted, then add an egg, beat up the whole thoroughly until well mixed; pour the mixture into a buttered tea-cup, tie it up in a small cloth as directed in the preceding Number, boil the pudding for twenty minutes, at least, and, as soon as done, turn it out on a plate. This, or any similar light kind of pudding, constitutes safe food for the most delicate.

No. 199. How to make a Tapioca Pudding.

Put two table-spoonfuls of tapioca into a basin with four lumps of sugar, a grain of salt, and a lump of sugar rubbed on the rind of a lemon; pour a gill of boiling milk over these ingredients and cover them up with a saucer to steep for ten minutes, then add one egg; beat up all together, and boil the pudding in a buttered tea-cup tied up in a cloth, for nearly half an hour.

No. 200. How to make an Arrow-root Pudding.

Mix a large dessert-spoonful of arrow-root with the same quantity of bruised sugar, and a tea-cupful of milk, in a small clean saucepan; stir this on the fire until it boils, and keep on stirring it, off the fire, for five minutes, until the heat has subsided; then add an egg, beat up and thoroughly mix it into the batter, and then boil the pudding as shown in the preceding Numbers.

No. 201. How to make a Sago Pudding.

Soak two table-spoonfuls of pearl sago with a tea-spoonful of hot milk, in a covered basin, for a quarter of an hour; then add a very little grated nutmeg or lemon-peel, sugar to sweeten, and an egg; beat up all together until thoroughly mixed, and then boil the pudding in a buttered basin or tea-cup, as directed in preceding cases.

No. 202. How to make a Ground-rice Pudding.

Mix a large table-spoonful of ground rice with half a pint of milk, six lumps of sugar, and a very little nutmeg; stir this in a saucepan on the fire until it has boiled for five minutes; then mix in an egg, and boil the pudding for twenty-five minutes.

No. 203. Brown and Polson Tea-cup Pudding for Infants.

Mix a good dessert-spoonful of Brown and Polson's corn-flour with half a pint of milk, six lumps of sugar, a grain of salt, and a very little grated orange-peel; stir these on the fire to boil for five minutes, then add one egg, beat up until well mixed; pour this batter into a buttered tea-cup, tie it up in a small cloth, boil it for twenty-five minutes, and serve it while hot.

———

MEDICINAL, HERBACEOUS, AND OTHER DRINKS FOR INVALIDS, ETC.

No. 204. BRAN TEA: A REMEDY FOR COLDS, ETC.

Boil a large handful of bran in a quart of water for ten minutes, then strain off the water into a jug, sweeten it with one ounce of gum arabic and a good spoonful of honey; stir all well together, and give this kind of drink in all cases of affections of the chest, such as colds, catarrhs, consumption, etc., and also for the measles.

No. 205. ORANGEADE, OR ORANGE DRINK.

Peel off the rind of one orange very thinly without any of the white pith, and put the rind into a jug; pare off all the white pith from three oranges so as to lay the pulp of the fruit quite bare, cut them in slices, take out all the seeds, or, as they are more generally termed, the pips, as their bitterness would render the drink unpalatable; add one ounce of sugar, or honey, pour a quart of boiling water to these, cover up the jug, and allow the orangeade to stand and steep until quite cold; it may then be given to the patient. This is a cooling beverage, and may be safely given in cases of fever.

No. 206. HOW TO MAKE LEMONADE.

Proceed in all particulars as directed for making orangeade, using, for the purpose, lemons instead of oranges.

No. 207. APPLE-WATER DRINK.

Slice up thinly three or four apples without peeling them, and boil them in a very clean saucepan with a quart of water and a little sugar until the slices of apples are become soft; the apple water must then be strained through a piece of clean muslin, or rag, into a jug. This pleasant beverage should be drunk when cold; it is considered beneficial in aiding to allay scorbutic eruptions.

No. 208. How to make a Soothing Drink for Coughs.

Take of marsh-mallow roots and of liquorice roots each one ounce; of linseed, half an ounce; shave the roots very thinly; put them and the linseed into a clean earthen pot with one quart of hot water, cover with the lid, and set the whole on the hob of the fire to simmer for half an hour or more; then strain the drink into a clean jug, sweeten with honey, and when it has become quite cold, let it be given in small quantities several times in the course of the day. This mucilaginous beverage is most beneficial in relieving persons who are suffering from cold on the chest, and also those who are afflicted with gravel, etc.

No. 209. Linseed Tea.

Put a table-spoonful of linseed into a clean earthen pot or pipkin with a quart of water, and a little orange or lemon rind; boil this gently for about ten minutes, and then strain it through muslin into a jug; sweeten with honey or sugar, add the juice of a lemon, stir all together, and give this beverage to allay irritation of the chest and lungs—in the latter case, the lemon juice had better be omitted. Linseed tea in its purest form is an excellent accessory in aiding to relieve such as are afflicted with gout, gravel, etc.

No. 210. Camomile Tea.

Put about thirty flowers into a jug, pour a pint of

boiling water upon them, cover up the tea, and when it has stood about ten minutes, pour it off from the flowers into another jug; sweeten with sugar or honey; drink a tea-cupful of it fasting in the morning to strengthen the digestive organs, and restore the liver to healthier action. A tea-cupful of camomile tea, in which is stirred a large dessert-spoonful of moist sugar, and a little grated ginger, is an excellent thing to administer to aged people a couple of hours before their dinner.

No. 211. BALM AND BURRAGE TEA.

These, as well as all other medicinal herbs, may easily be cultivated in a corner of your garden, when you are so fortunate as to live in a cottage of your own in the country; they are also to be obtained from all herbalists in large towns. Take of balm and burrage a small handful each, put this into a jug, pour in upon the herbs a quart of boiling water, allow the tea to stand for ten minutes, and then strain it off into another jug, and let it become cold. This cooling drink is recommended as a beverage for persons whose system has become heated from any cause.

No. 212. SAGE OR MARYGOLD TEA.

Put a dozen sage leaves into a tea-pot, pour boiling water upon them, and, after allowing the tea to stand for five or ten minutes, it may be drunk with sugar and milk, in the same way and instead of the cheaper kinds of teas, which are sold for foreign teas, but which are too often composed of some kind of leaf more or less resembling the real plant, without any of its genuine fragrance, and are, from their spurious and almost poisonous nature, calculated to produce evil to all who consume them, besides the drawback of their being expensive articles.

Teas made from sage leaves, dried mint, marygolds,

and more particularly the leaf of the black currant tree, form a very pleasant as well as wholesome kind of beverage; and, if used in equal proportions, would be found to answer very well as a most satisfactory substitute for bad and expensive tea.

No. 213. How to Stew Red Cabbages.

The use of the red cabbage in this country is confined to its being pickled almost raw, and eaten in that detestable and injurious state, whereby its anti-scorbutic powers are annulled.

The red cabbage, when merely boiled with bacon, or with a little butter and salt, is both nutritious and beneficial in a medicinal point of view, inasmuch as that it possesses great virtue in all scorbutic and dartrous affections. On the Continent it is customary to administer it in such cases in the form of a syrup, and also in a gelatinized state. The red cabbage, stewed in the following manner, will be found a very tasty dish :—Slice up the red cabbage rather thin, wash it well, drain it, and then put it into a saucepan with a little dripping or butter, a gill of vinegar, pepper and salt ; put the lid on, and set the cabbage to stew slowly on the hob, stirring it occasionally from the bottom to prevent it from burning ; about an hour's gentle stewing will suffice to cook it thoroughly. All kinds of cabbage or kail are anti-scorbutic agents.

No. 214. How to make Toast Water.

Toast a piece of bread thoroughly browned to its centre without being *burnt*, put it into a jug, pour boiling water upon it, cover over and allow it to stand and steep until it has cooled ; it will then be fit to drink.

No. 215. How to make Barley Water.

Boil one ounce of barley in a quart of water for

twenty minutes ; strain through muslin into a jug
containing a bit of orange or lemon peel.

No. 216. How to make Rice Water.

To six ounces of rice add two quarts of water, and
two ounces of Valentia raisins; boil these very gently
for about half an hour, or rather more ; strain off the
water into a jug, add about two table-spoonfuls of
brandy. Rice water, prepared as above, is recommended in cases of dysentery and diarrhœa.

No. 217. How to make Treacle Posset.

Sweeten a pint of milk with four table-spoonfuls
of treacle, boil this for ten minutes ; strain it through
a rag; drink it while hot, and go to bed well covered
with blankets; and your cold will be all the less and
you the better for it.

No. 218. How to make White Wine Whey.

Put a pint of milk into a very clean saucepan or
skillet, to boil on the fire; then add half a gill of any
kind of white wine; allow the milk to boil up, then
pour it into a basin, and allow it to stand in a cool
place, that the curd may fall to the bottom of the
basin ; then pour off the whey—which is excellent as
an agent to remove a severe cough or cold.

No. 219. How to make a Cordial for Colds.

First, prepare a quart of the juice of black currants, by bruising and boiling them for twenty
minutes, and then straining off the juice with great
pressure through a sieve into a basin. Next, boil
four ounces of linseed in a quart of water until reduced
to one-third of its original quantity, taking care that
it does not boil fast, and, when done, strain the liquid
into a very clean saucepan; add the currant juice, two
pounds of moist sugar, and half an ounce of citric

acid, or one pint of lemon juice; boil all together until reduced to a thick syrup—that is, when it begins to run rather thick from the spoon without resembling treacle; as soon as the syrup has reached this stage, remove it from the fire, and pour it into a jug to become quite cold. This syrup will keep good for any length of time, if bottled and corked down tight, and kept in a cool place. A tea-spoonful taken occasionally will soon relieve the most troublesome cough.

This cordial may also be prepared in winter, using for the purpose black currant jam, or preserved black currant juice, instead of the juice of fresh-gathered currants.

No. 220. How to make a Stringent Gargle.

Put the following ingredients into a very clean earthen pipkin:—Twenty sage leaves, a handful of red rose leaves, and a pint of water; boil these for twenty minutes, then add a gill of vinegar, and two table-spoonfuls of honey; boil again for ten minutes, and strain the gargle through a muslin rag, to be used when cold.

No. 221. A Simple Remedy against Wind on the Stomach.

A few drops (say four) of essence of peppermint on a lump of sugar.

No. 222. A Cure for a Hard Dry Cough.

Take of each one table-spoonful — spermaceti grated, honey, and peppermint water; mix all together with the yolks of two eggs in a gallipot. A tea-spoonful to be taken on the tongue, and allowed to be swallowed slowly as it dissolves.

No. 223. A Cooling Drink.

To half an ounce of cream of tartar, add one ounce

of loaf sugar, and a bit of orange or lemon peel; put these into a jug, pour upon them a quart of boiling water; stir all together, and allow the beverage to become cold.

No. 224. Hop Tea.

Pour a quart of boiling water upon half an ounce of hops, cover this over, and allow the infusion to stand for fifteen minutes; the tea must then be strained off into another jug. A small tea-cupful may be drunk fasting in the morning, which will create an appetite, and also strengthen the digestive organs.

No. 225. Lime-flower Tea.

To half an ounce of lime-flowers, placed in a tea-pot or jug, pour a pint of boiling water, and when the infusion has stood for ten minutes, sweeten with honey or sugar, and drink the tea hot, to assuage the pains in the stomach and chest, arising from indigestion. This beverage may also be successfully administered in attacks of hysteria.

No. 226. Hyssop Tea: a Remedy for Worms.

To a quarter of an ounce of dried hyssop flowers, pour one pint of boiling water; allow the tea to infuse for ten minutes, pour it off, sweeten with honey, and take a wine-glassful three times in the course of the day; this will prove an effectual cure when children are troubled with worms.

No. 227. Iceland Moss Jelly.

Boil four ounces of Iceland moss in one quart of water very slowly for one hour, then add the juice of two lemons and a bit of rind, four ounces of sugar, and a gill of sherry; boil up, and remove the scum from the surface; strain the jelly through a muslin bag into a basin, and set it aside to become cold; in which state it may be eaten, but it is far more efficacious in its beneficial results when taken warm. The use of Iceland moss jelly is strongly recommended in cases of consumption, and in the treatment of severe colds, catarrhs, and all phlegmatic diseases of the chest.

No. 228. Antispasmodic Tea.

Infuse two-pennyworth of hay saffron (sold at all chemists') in a gill of boiling water in a tea-cup for ten minutes; add a dessert-spoonful of brandy, and sugar to sweeten, and drink the tea hot. This powerful yet harmless remedy will quickly relieve you from spasmodic pains occasioned by indigestion.

No. 229. Dandelion Tea.

Infuse one ounce of dandelion in a jug with a pint of boiling water for fifteen minutes; sweeten with brown sugar or honey, and drink several tea-cupfuls during the day. The use of this tea is recommended as a safe remedy in all bilious affections; it is also an excellent beverage for persons afflicted with dropsy.

No. 230. Refreshing Drink for Sore Throat attended with Fever.

Boil two ounces of barberries with half an ounce of violets in a quart of water for ten minutes; sweeten with honey, strain off into a jug, and drink several glasses during the day.

No. 231. A Cure for Sprains.

Bruise thoroughly a handful of sage-leaves, and boil them in a gill of vinegar for ten minutes, or until reduced to half the original quantity; apply this in a folded rag to the part affected, and tie it on securely with a bandage.

No. 232. A Cure for Chilblains.

The pulp of a baked turnip beat up in a tea-cup

G

with a table-spoonful of salad oil, ditto of mustard, and ditto of scraped horse-radish; apply this mixture to the chilblains, and tie it on with a piece of rag.

No. 233. A Cure for Burns or Scalds.

Thoroughly bruise a raw onion and a potato into a pulp, by scraping or beating them with a rolling-pin; mix this pulp with a good table-spoonful of salad oil, and apply it to the naked burn or scald; secure it on the part with a linen bandage.

No. 234. A Cure for Cold in the Head.

Thirty drops of camphorated sal volatile in a small wine-glassful of hot water, taken several times in the course of the day.

No. 235. A Cure for the Sting of Wasps or Bees.

Bruise the leaf of the poppy, and apply it to the part affected.

No. 236. A Cure for Toothache.

Roll a small bit of cotton wadding into a ball the size of a pea, dip this in a very few drops of camphorated chloroform, and with it fill the hollow part of the decayed tooth.

No. 237. How to make Coffee.

Mix one ounce of ground coffee in a clean pot with a pint of cold water, stir this on the fire till it boils, then throw in a very little more cold water, and after allowing the coffee to boil up twice more, set it aside to settle, and become clear and bright. The dregs saved from twice making, added to half the quantity of fresh coffee, will do for the children. It is best to make your coffee over-night, as it has then plenty of time to settle. If, as I recommend, you grind your coffee at home, you will find Nye's machines very good.

No. 238. How to Prepare Cocoa Nibs.

Boil gently two ounces of cocoa nibs in three pints of water for two hours and a-half, without allowing it to reduce more than one-third; that is, the three pints should be boiled down to one quart. When sufficiently boiled, strain the cocoa from the nibs, mix it with equal proportions of milk, and sweeten with sugar. Two ounces of cocoa nibs cost a penny three-farthings, one quart of skim milk twopence (in the country one penny), two ounces of moist sugar three farthings; thus, for about fourpence halfpenny, you may prepare sufficient cocoa for the breakfasts of four persons. This would be much wholesomer and cheaper than tea. To be sure, it would take some trouble and care to prepare it, and this should be attended to over-night.

No. 239. ECONOMICAL AND SUBSTANTIAL SOUP FOR DISTRIBUTION TO THE POOR.

I am well aware, from my own experience, that the charitable custom of distributing wholesome and nutritious soup to poor families living in the immediate neighbourhood of noblemen and gentlemen's mansions in the country, already exists to a great extent; yet, it is certainly desirable that this excellent practice should become more generally adopted, especially during the winter months, when their scanty means of subsistence but insufficiently yield them food adequate in quantity to sustain the powers of life in a condition equal to their hard labour. To afford the industrious well-deserving poor a little assistance in this way, would call forth their gratitude to the givers, and confer a blessing on the needy. The want of knowing how to properly prepare the kind of soup best adapted to the purpose has, no doubt, in a great measure, militated against its being more generally bestowed throughout the kingdom; and it is in order to supply that deficient knowledge, that I have determined on giving easy instructions for its preparation.

No. 240. How to Prepare a Large Quantity of Good Soup for the Poor.

It is customary with most large families, while living in the country, to kill at least some portion of the meat consumed in their households; and without supposing for a moment that any portion of this is ever wasted, I may be allowed to suggest that certain parts, such as sheep's heads, plucks, shanks, and scrag-ends, might very well be spared towards making a good mess of soup for the poor. The bones left from cooked joints, first baked in a brisk oven for a quarter of an hour, and afterwards boiled in a large copper of water for six hours, would readily prepare a gelatinized foundation broth for the soup; the bones, when sufficiently boiled, to be taken out. And thus, supposing that your copper is already part filled with the broth made from bones (all the grease having been removed from the surface), add any meat you may have, cut up in pieces of about four ounces weight, garnish plentifully with carrots, celery, onions, some thyme, and ground allspice, well-soaked split peas, barley, or rice; and, as the soup boils up, skim it well occasionally, season moderately with salt, and after about four hours' gentle and continuous boiling, the soup will be ready for distribution. It was the custom in families where I have lived as cook, to allow a pint of this soup, served out with the pieces of meat in it, to as many as the recipients' families numbered; and the soup was made for distribution twice every week during winter.

No. 241. Another Method for making Economical Soup.

In households where large joints of salt beef, or pork, are cooked almost daily for the family, the liquor in which they have been boiled should be saved, all grease removed therefrom, put into the copper with a plentiful supply of carrots, parsnips, celery, and onions, all cut in small pieces, the whole boiled and well skimmed till the vegetables are done; the soup is then to be thickened with either oatmeal, pease-meal, or Indian corn meal, seasoned with pepper and ground allspice, and stirred continuously until it boils up again; it must then be skimmed, and the best pieces of meat selected from the stock-pot should be kept in careful reserve, to be added to the soup, and allowed to boil therein for half an hour longer.

No. 242. How to make Fish Soup in Large Quantities for Distribution to the Poor.

This kind of soup, it will be easily understood, is applicable only on the sea-coast, and wherever fish is to be had very cheap. Chop fine a dozen onions, some thyme, and winter savory, and put these in a copper, or some large pot, with about six gallons of water, one pound of butter, pepper and salt enough to season; allow the whole to boil for ten minutes, then thicken the broth with about four pounds of oatmeal, pease-meal, or flour; stir the soup continuously until it boils, and then throw in about fifteen pounds of fish cut up in one-pound size pieces, and also some chopped parsley; boil all together until the fish is done, and then serve out the soup to the recipients. All kinds of fish, except sprats, herrings, and pilchards, are equally well adapted for making fish soup, but codfish, cod's heads, skate, eels, etc., and all glutinous fish, suit the purpose best.

INDEX.

THE END.

Thomas Harrild, Printer, Shoe Lane, Fleet Street, London.

CHARLES ELMÉ FRANCATELLI

Charles Elmé Francatelli (1805 - 1876) was born in London in 1805 of Italian ancestry, but his culinary art was learnt in France.

He was chef de cuisine to several top Victorian families before managing Crockfords and the St James Club. He later became maitre d'hotel to the royal household and Chief Cook in Ordinary to Queen Victoria.

He was a very successful author. His THE MODERN COOK was first published in 1845 and went through twelve editions. In 1861, the year in which he published THE COOK'S GUIDE AND BUTLER'S ASSISTANT, he also issued his PLAIN COOKERY BOOK FOR THE WORKING CLASSES.

The Dictionary of National Biography calls Francatelli a culinary economist, and he once said that he could feed a thousand families a day on the food that was wasted in London.

OTHER BOOKS AVAILABLE
FROM PRYOR PUBLICATIONS

CROSSE and BLACKWELL, Purveyors in Ordinary to Her Majesty, in soliciting attention to the above extract, beg to state that the utmost care is taken to insure purity and wholesomeness in their various productions. Their Establishment has been inspected by Dr. HASSALL, and many leading Members of the Medical Profession, who have been pleased to express their high approval of the General Manufacturing arrangements. Every article prepared by C. and B. is of the highest quality that can be produced, their PICKLES, TARTS, FRUITS, AND PRESERVES, are perfectly natural in Colour; no mineral or other deleterious ingredient being employed to give them an undue brilliancy.

C. and B. respectfully invite attention to the following, all of which are particularly recommended.

PICKLES of various kinds: prepared in pure malt vinegar.

BOTTLED FRUITS, FOR TARTS AND PUDDINGS; preserved in their natural state.

JELLIES of unequalled brilliancy and purity; consisting of Calf's Foot, Orange, Lemon, Noyau, Punch, Madeira, etc. In pint and quart bottles for the convenience of Families.

ROYAL TABLE SAUCE; of a warm and delicious flavour, peculiarly adapted for cold meats, and greatly improving hashes, stews, and made dishes.

ESSENCE of ANCHOVIES; produced solely from the REAL GORGONA ANCHOVIES, and superior to all other preparations sold under the same name.

ESSENCE of SHRIMPS; manufactured on the sea-coast where the Shrimps are caught. This Sauce being milder in flavour than the Essence of Anchovies, is preferred by many epicures.

THE CELEBRATED SOHO SAUCE; for Game, Venison, etc.

PURE MUSHROOM CATSUP; made from the finest Mushrooms obtained on the famed Leicestershire Downs.

SIR ROBERT PEEL'S SAUCE; for general purposes, manufactured by J. Carstairs, Edinburgh. Each bottle bears a fac-simile of the late Right Hon. Baronet's letter of approval.

ANCHOVY PASTE, BLOATER PASTE, STRASBOURG and other POTTED MEATS: for the Breakfast and Luncheon Table.

ORANGE MARMALADE, JAMS, and JELLIES; perfectly pure and prepared by a process which effectually retains the fine aroma of the Fruit.

Of MARMALADE the "Lancet" of 22nd January, 1853, remarks, "6th Sample, purchased of CROSSE and BLACKWELL, 21, Soho Square. Ash of a yellow colour; does not contain COPPER.

C. and B. are also Wholesale Agents for M. SOYER'S SAUCES, RELISH, and AROMATIC MUSTARD, all of which the 'Lancet' declares to be pure: for Barrie and Co.'s Curry and Mulligatawny Paste and Chattny's, which are shipped direct from Madras; also for Payne's Royal Osborne Sauce; and for Lea and Perrin's Worcestershire Sauce.

The above, together with all their other Condiments and Delicacies, may be obtained of most respectable Sauce Vendors in the United Kingdom, at the principal Stores in India, America, and the Colonies, and wholesale of

CROSSE AND BLACKWELL,

BY SPECIAL APPOINTMENT PURVEYORS TO THE QUEEN,

21, SOHO SQUARE, LONDON.

Alexandra Elizabeth
Mathieson 6T
Thursday 12th September